Also by HARRY DRURY

Walking in the Cotswolds (Robert Hale 1981)

A Viennese Snuffbox (Robert Hale 1984)

Favourite Cotswold Walks

by

Harry Drury

RUSHMERE WYNNE

England

ISBN 0 948035 01 3

Photographs by Rex Haggett ARPS

Cover photographs from top to bottom are:
Duntisbourne Rouse Church (Walk Eleven)
The Windrush Valley (Walk Six)
Painswick Valley (Walk Nine)

Published by:
Rushmere Wynne Ltd.
P.O. Box 491, Leighton Buzzard,
Bedfordshire LU7 7WQ

Printed by:
RaynerPrint Ltd.
Buzzard Works, Billington Road,
Leighton Buzzard, Beds. LU7 8IN

Typesetting by:
LB Print Services (0525) 850806

Design by:
Alan James (0525) 851957

PLEASE OBSERVE THE COUNTRY CODE

Guard against fire risk

Fasten all gates

Keep dogs under proper control

Keep to the paths across farmland

Avoid damaging fences, hedges and walls

Leave no litter

Safeguard water supplies

Protect wild life, wild plants and trees

Go carefully on country roads

Respect the life of the countryside

PUBLISHER'S NOTE

KEY TO ROUTE MAPS

Letters on maps relating to information in script	A
Direction Post	DP
Yellow Arrow	YA
Stile	S
Gate	G
Cotswold Way sign	CW
Sign post	SP
Blue arrow (Bridle path)	BA
Trees and woods	shaded
Kissing gate	KG
National Trust	NT
Public footpath	PF
Way mark	W

THE COTSWOLDS
— showing the starting point
of the fifteen walks

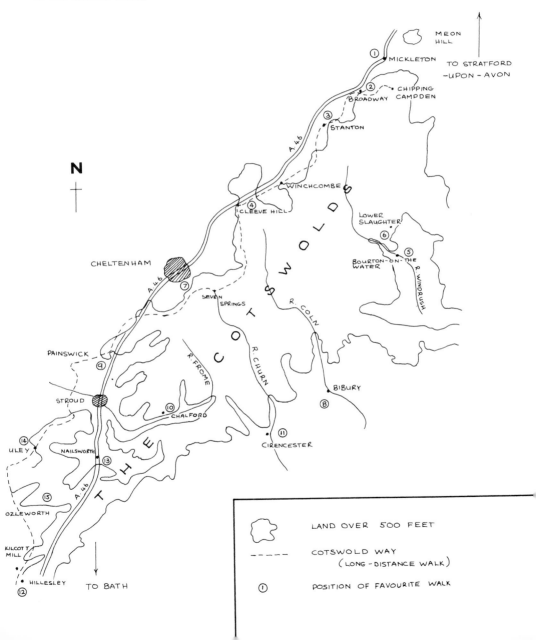

INTRODUCTION

The forerunner of this book was published in 1981, ten years ago, and as far as I know it was the first comprehensive book of walks on the Cotswold Hills. It was entitled 'Walking in the Cotswolds' and comprised 41 major walks, and 100 short and longer variations. It has been gratifying to the author to learn how much pleasure it has brought to large numbers of walkers — some of them doing the 100-mile, long distance Cotswold Way from Chipping Campden to Bath. Visiting walkers from America, Australia, New Zealand and Europe have conveyed expressions of enjoyment, which has made all the arduous work undertaken for its production worth while.

However, after the passing of a decade there have been many changes on the routes — particularly the Cotswold Way, and the book is beginning to get out of date, so it has been decided to discontinue publication and consider a successor.

My new publishers have come up with an interesting idea which, after due consideration and negotiation, has resolved itself into the choice of the author's favourite walks on the lovely Cotswold Hills. Fifteen have been selected, all of which have been re-walked during the first half of 1991, carefully mapped and described and supported with some historic and explanatory insets. They are all circular routes, except one, so that transport is eased. The average length is around eight miles which is a reasonable distance for the ordinary walker.

The Cotswold Hills stretch for 100 miles from Meon Hill at Mickleton in the north to Bath at the southern end and are a unique range. The jurassic limestone of which they are composed has produced a stone unlike anything else in Britain, which has characteristics that have made possible the creation of glorious villages like Chipping Campden, Broadway and Stanton. Cotswold stone is easy to work, is in abundant supply and has the special nature of getting steadily harder the longer it is exposed to the atmosphere, so that the stone cottages and buildings in the High Street at Chipping Campden are in perfect condition after 600 years of existence. In addition to this quality it is lovely visually — originally golden, honey-shaded then mellowing to a pale grey . . . no wonder the High Street is world-famous for its beauty. Not surprising, also, that Christopher Wren used stone from the quarries at Taynton, Burford, when building the interior of St. Paul's Cathedral.

This range of hills has another special quality. It produces pasture on its soft rolling slopes that is ideal for rearing sheep. In the Middle Ages it was the prime region for the production of wool in Europe, and its merchants became very wealthy. They tended to lavish their affluence on the great churches that can be found in Cotswold villages, magnificent cathedral-like structures such as you will find in Northleach, Painswick and Chipping Campden. So, stone and wool and natural beauty have combined to make a wonderland, which Shakespeare must have known.

The Cotswold Hills are not high, 1,083 feet at Cleeve Hill being the maximum, but there are some quite stiff climbs in places and walkers are certainly advised to wear good, sturdy, walking boots for your journeys, carrying waterproofs and drinks in your haversacks for they will be valuable when miles away out on the hills. Important, too, is the recommendation that you carry a compass for, though the maps in this book are accurate and explicit, it is all too easy to go to the wrong corner of a sixty-acre field and add half a mile to your walk!

The maps and script should be all you need, but it is always helpful to back them up with the appropriate Ordnance Survey map of the area. The 1:50,000 scales have long been in use, but the larger-scale 1:25,000 (2½ inches to the mile) now cover most of the Cotswolds. On these, hedges are marked and public rights of way are shown in green dotted lines.

I have tried to ensure that all the walks are on public rights of way, or on paths where passage is permitted by the owners, but no responsibility attaches to the publishers if I should have erred anywhere. Farmers can be helpful, but some are most obstructive and occasionally you will find paths over fields have been obliterated by ploughing and planting. This sometimes happens with paths alongside hedges, so that one may have to cross a field through mud. I think considerate farmers predominate, but in any case please have regard for the Country Code — particulary remembering to close gates behind you.

The Cotswolds are rich in history, some of which is recounted in this book . . . neolithic man had seventeen hill-forts on its heights (such as Uleybury and Shenberrow) — the Romans left plenty of evidence of their occupation at Chedworth and elsewhere — the Normans were at Avening, Cirencester and many other spots, and one of the oldest remains of ancient man can be seen at Belas Knap above Winchcombe (it is at least 5,000 years old).

As you walk the hills and pass the villages you will be reminded, too, that many famous people have lived where they had humble beginnings . . . William Tyndale who first gave us the New Testament in our native tongue, Dr. Jenner who discovered vaccination, William Morris (who pioneered arts and crafts), Edward Burne-Jones the painter, John Keeble and Graham Greene, the author.

So, as you get away from the noise and turmoil of life in the towns into the quiet of the Cotswold Hills it is hoped you will derive infinite pleasure on these walks in keeping the body healthy and the mind enchanted. There are beautiful woods to experience and wild flowers are abundant. I have seen a kestrel in Papermill valley, a kingfisher along Ozleworth Bottom and a plover on my way to Blockley.

In the main the Cotswold Way walk follows the western escarpment, with superb views over the river estuary and the Welsh mountains. I have done the long-distance walk four times and I never tire of its delights. The big walk is not covered in this book but many of the fifteen walks selected take in parts of the Cotswold Way, which might motivate you to tackle the 100-mile route.

The selection of fifteen favourite walks is a very subjective matter, especially as there are said to be 1,600 miles of public footpaths on the Cotswold Hills. I have tried to spread my choice over the whole range (except the extreme south, where the hills begin to vanish), bearing in mind the attractiveness, beauty and interest of each route chosen. Where possible I have borne in mind the position of inns for refreshment, and always endeavoured to choose walks bearing items of interest.

In wishing you every enjoyment I would like to express my warm thanks to the team of walkers who have accompanied me during the past six months, especially Alfred Newman, my companion and artist friend when 'Walking in the Cotswolds' was being prepared, and in particular Elsie, my wife, for her unstinting support and forbearance.

Harry Drury

CONTENTS

WALK ONE

Mickleton: Circular Route via Chipping Campden

Distance: 8½ miles

Often described as the most northerly Cotswold village, Mickleton is scarcely typical because of modern development on its outskirts, and the constant traffic through it on the B.4632 road. Nevertheless, the centre round the Victorian memorial fountain, the site of the Manor House, and the church merit some attention before one passes on to the hills (A).

> **B.** Mickleton had a church in Saxon times around 960, during the reign of King Edgar. The present parish church of St Lawrence was begun at the time of Henry II, records showing its first rector in 1180. Its unusual broach spire (one rising from the tower without a parapet) was added in 1352. Note the delightful Upper Room, which served as a school for poor boys from 1665 until 1857. There are memorials to the Graves family who owned the adjoining Manor, which also saw the birth of the celebrated Endymion Porter, patron of poets and the arts and courtier to James I and Charles I. The 100-year-old clock, which has a most pleasant chime, used to be wound daily by the 'tower captain', a function now fallen into abeyance.

The walk moves off south-east over two fields, when you will see the ground rising steeply ahead, with trees appearing on the right. Crossing a stile, the path now lies through what was once a great avenue of majestic elms (C). Alas, they have all fallen victims to the Dutch elm disease. Until a few years ago the stumps were still visible, but they have now been removed. Down this colonnade the people from Hidcote Bartrim used to come to church on Sundays, when everybody worshipped at St Lawrence. There is now a short, sharp climb, keeping the property boundaries on your left, until you reach the road through a gate in the stone wall. Turn left into the grounds of Kiftsgate Court.

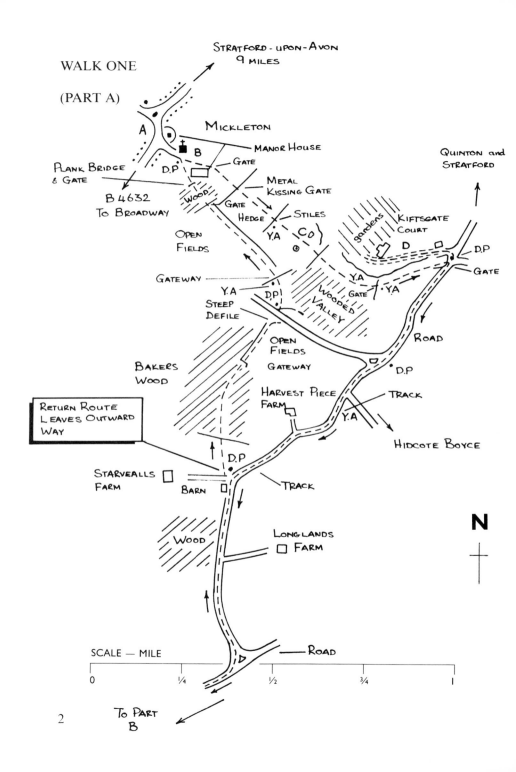

WALK ONE

(PART A)

STRATFORD-UPON-AVON
9 MILES

A

MICKLETON

MANOR HOUSE

B

PLANK BRIDGE
& GATE

D.P.

GATE

QUINTON and
STRATFORD

B 4632
TO BROADWAY

WOOD

GATE

METAL
KISSING GATE

HEDGE

STILES

Y.A

C

gardens

KIFTSGATE
COURT

D

D.P.

GATE

OPEN
FIELDS

GATEWAY

Y.A

Y.A

GATE

Y.A

STEEP
DEFILE

D.P.

WOODED
VALLEY

ROAD

OPEN
FIELDS

BAKERS
WOOD

GATEWAY

D.P.

RETURN ROUTE
LEAVES OUTWARD
WAY

HARVEST PIECE
FARM

TRACK

Y.A

HIDCOTE BOYCE

STARVEALLS
FARM

D.P.

BARN

TRACK

LONGLANDS
FARM

WOOD

N

SCALE — MILE

ROAD

0   ¼   ½   ¾   1

2

TO PART
B

D. Kiftsgate Court was built between 1887 and 1891 by Sidney Graves Hamilton, who owned the Manor House at Mickleton. The Court is now partially occupied by the Binny family, though the owner Mrs D. H. Binny lives in the Lodge at the entrance. The beautiful gardens are open to the public between April and September each year, and you are strongly advised to spare the time looking round, for the blaze of colour is worth travelling many miles to see.

Turn right as you leave and continue along the road. After a third of a mile you will pass the turning to Mickleton on your right, and shortly beyond the road turns sharp left to Hidcote Boyce and Ebrington. Here you go straight ahead on a track marked 'Unsuitable for motorists'. Follow this track for about a mile, passing three farms, until you reach a road, where the way lies to the right.

You will shortly pass on your left the drive to Mickleton Hills Farm (where the return walk emerges) but you continue to follow the road in a westerly direction. Notice on the right and left mounds of earth which were removed when Campden Tunnel was excavated. In a third of a mile turn sharp left at a direction post over a stile and go down the right-hand side of the field hedge. At the bottom cross a footbridge, turn right and pass a tiny pool. You then mount rising ground and will soon be rewarded by views of Campden church as you move southwards.

Passing barns on your right and left and crossing a stile you will now reach the playing fields of Campden School. Follow the path down the left-hand side of the fence till you turn sharp right at the bottom to enter an alley along the front of the school. It then turns left along iron railings, coming out in front of the magnificent church of Chipping Campden.

E. The parish church, whose superb tower can be seen for miles from every direction, is worthy to be called a cathedral. It is a product of the wealth and commitment of the 'wool kings' of the Middle Ages who lavished their money on the Cotswold churches.

Chipping Campden church is an epic poem in stone with so much craftsmanship and history embedded in its great nave, aisles, chapels, chancel and tower that it is impossible here in brevity to make selections. You Cotswold walkers are urged to spend a while within and offer a prayer.

The church occupies the site of earlier churches. What is here now is almost entirely fifteenth century, built in the heyday of Perpendicular style. William Grevel, whose thirteenth-century house still stands in the High Street (F) a monument to the great 'wool king', probably played the major part in the erection of this famous church, whose completion came with the creation of the 120ft tower in the year 1500. Another generous benefactor to the church and town was Sir Baptist Hicks (later to become Viscount Campden) who in 1612 presented the beautiful pulpit and later the Flemish-made brass lectern. Effigies of him and his wife can be seen in the South Chapel.

It may now be convenient for you to stop for lunch at one of the many inns or restaurants available. William Morris and G. M. Trevelyan lavished high praise on this famous street whose Cotswold stone houses are as much as 600 years old. Do not fail to see the Wool Market which has an international reputation.

G. The Wool Market (also known as the Market Hall) is an epitome of the history of the town, because the Cotswolds are bound up with sheep, wool and oolitic limestone. This old building, standing so majestically there, right in the centre of the High Street, has caught the eye of a constant stream of visitors, and at least one American wanted to buy it, dismantle its stonework and cart it off to the New World for re-erection! It was built in 1627 by Sir Baptist Hicks, who became the first Lord Campden and remained in possession of the family until 1942 when it was purchased by the National Trust.

The walk retraces the outward route back to the path along the side of the

Chipping Campden High Street ('the most beautiful street in Europe') with its famous Wool Market. (G)

(PART B)

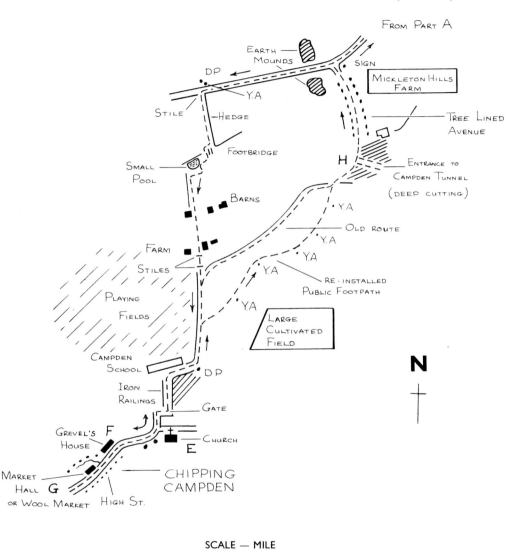

SCALE — MILE

0   ¼   ½   ¾   1

school playing fields where one reaches a huge cultivated field. Nine or ten years ago the farmer moved the public footpath from across the centre of the field to the northern edge where it ran alongside the hedge, and has become a pleasant grassy path. Now that it has become part of the Heart-of-England Way the authorities have put it back to its original position across the centre of the field and marked it with direction posts. Unfortunately it has not been properly made and is just a muddy morass, which will be most unattractive to hikers. Until it is improved I can see many walkers going round the grass path.

   At the far end cross a stile, veer right and go past Mickleton Hills Farm. Just this side of the farm you can look down through the trees to see the railway cutting and the entrance to Campden Tunnel (H).

Baker's Wood — with its lovely beech trees.

H. The tunnel was built around 1851, mainly by Irish navvies, to make possible the laying of the main line from London to Worcester. It is interesting that it was sited so that the station is one mile from the village ensuring that the heritage of Chipping Campden was not imperilled.

The walk proceeds up the farm drive through a beautiful avenue of magnificent trees to the road where we join the outward route and follow the track back to Starvealls Farm. At the barn turn left and almost immediately right where there is a yellow arrow and Heart-of-England Way sign, the pathway lying to the left of the hedge. After about 150 yards we enter Baker's Wood, running along the top of Baker's Hill.

The wood stretches for nearly half a mile, the last 250 yards of which is across an open field. You descend to the road through a small, steep defile. Cross the road and bear left over a wooden gate, heading over the field to a gateway in the far hedge. You will see the spire of Mickleton church ahead. Cross the next field keeping to the left of the hedge, and go through a gate into a path through a small wood. The route leaves the wood over a plank bridge and gate, from which you make for the left side of the stone wall ahead, and you will find yourself back at the starting point by the church.

Alternatives:

la **3 mile walk.** Mickleton — Kiftsgate Court — along track to Starvealls Farm, and back through Baker's Wood.

lb **2 miles.** Mickleton to Kiftsgate Court and back.

lc **3 miles.** From Chipping Campden take the inward part of the main walk to Mickleton Hills Farm, then turn left where the tree-lined avenue hits the road. then follow outward route back to Chipping Campden.

ld If you have two cars you can do half the main walk from Mickleton to Chipping Campden or vice versa. **Distance 4 miles.**

Parking:

A number of cars can be parked in the drive road at Mickleton leading from the B.4632 to the church.

At Chipping Campden you will probably find a place in the High Street, but if not you can park in Calf Lane, parallel to High Street.

WALK TWO

Broadway:
Circular Walk via Saintbury
and Broadway Tower

Distance: 8½ miles

This walk is centred on the village of Broadway, one of the show places in all England. It lies cradled in the high hills of the northern Cotswolds, and for this reason Walk Two involves some climbing. Of the thousands of visitors who come all year round to this most popular spot in the lovely Cotswold hills only a small fraction take advantage of the delightful pathways where one can feel the pleasure of the rich green turf, fill the lungs with clear fresh air and enjoy spectacular views along the many walks available. It is lacking in discernment to concentrate on all the antique shops and eating places and overlook the joy of rambling in these hills.

The trail now described is really two shorter walks which are combined to make one longer route taking in some of the most attractive features of the area. It starts at the car park at the northern end of the village just along the turning to Stratford-upon-Avon. The path goes past the toilets onto a minor road where you turn left and go straight ahead till you reach two houses named 'Salubrious'. Turn left and continue along an alley, crossing a small road on the way. After some 200 yards cross a footbridge where a track goes left to Hill Farm. A gate leads into fields and shortly a stile marks the divergence of two paths. Take the left-hand one which heads N.N.E. into an orchard.

The path now continues alongside a wood on the right and will soon reach a metalled road which you will follow for half a mile, passing the vehicle park and buildings of the Group 4 Security headquarters. At the end you will cross a minor road into fields from where the spire of Saintbury church can be seen. The directions on the map will lead you without difficulty to this landmark.

A. The tall spire of St. Nicholas, Saintbury is visible for miles, and is unusual

8

SCALE — MILE

0   ¼   ½   ¾   1

in that it comprises both a tower and a spire. An interesting feature is the early mass dial above the south doorway. The architecture is Norman and Perpendicular, showing work of different periods. It is worth taking time to inspect a thousand year old church.

Leave at the rear, and immediately undertake a steep climb to the hill top. Over to your right can be seen what is left of the ramparts of an Iron Age Hill Fort (B).

Proceed southwards over the fields, cross a lane and enter a bridle track which runs for half a mile along the north-western edge of Broadway Golf Course (C). Make sure you do not stray onto the course fairways, always staying on the track with the wire fence running on your immediate right.

Leave the golf course by a steep drop through two gates into fields which provide the path moving downhill until you join the outward path at point D. Retrace your steps back to the car park where the start was made.

E. The fine, long and wide main street of Broadway, with its well-kept green verges, is a truly eye-catching vista of old stone houses built chiefly in the 17th and 18th centuries of the lovely honey-coloured oolitic limestone which has contributed so significantly to the unique qualities of the Cotswolds. No wonder that summer and winter it is always thronged with visitors from all over the world.

The main street of Broadway was not always sited where it is at present, as evidenced by the position of the original parish church — St Eadburgh's — which is nearly a mile down the Snowshill Road, and is isolated and seldom used. The village of old was once clustered round that church, and the coach road from London to Worcester went up Conygree Lane, a mile to the east of the main road that now winds its way up Fish Hill.

The ancient Beaker people who settled here from the European continent before the Romans came would have been puzzled, indeed, if they could have conceived of the fame of what the early Cotsaerils called 'Broddy'.

There certainly is some special quality that draws folk to this well-known village.

Before you take lunch or a snack at one of the many inns or restaurants it is suggested that you stroll down the famous High Street as far as the modern parish church, noticing on the right the world-famous Lygon Arms Hotel (F), where — strange to relate — an ancestor of the writer was manager in the early 1800s.

The walk so far will have taken you some four and a half miles, and it is hoped that fortified with refreshment the second part will beckon with

Broadway — gem of the Cotswolds

attraction. It starts in the same place as the first section — i.e. the car park at the northern end of the village.

This time after passing behind the toilets the way lies straight over the first road, through an alleyway to turn left on the main A44 Oxford road which proceeds up Fish Hill.

Go along the side of this main road for about a quarter of a mile until you reach Pike Cottage. Turn left over a stone stile at a direction post marked 'Chipping Campden' and follow uphill by the side of iron railings for 350 yards until you come to a stile. Pass the stile and a clap gate just beyond and continue uphill in an easterly direction, keeping the hedge on your right. Shortly the path becomes a stone track which stretches for about 300 yards until it ends with open fields. The route continues eastwards and you climb towards the ridge ahead. Pass a spring, a stile and a direction post before reaching Green Lane at the top.

Go over the road where there is a direction post into the woods. Mount some steps and turn to a southerly pointing path which proceeds for a third of a mile through some very delightful woodland scenery. This eventually comes out at the main road at the top of Fish Hill, and here you meet and for a while travel on the long-distance Cotswold Way.

Cross over the road and follow for half a mile a delightful route through

11

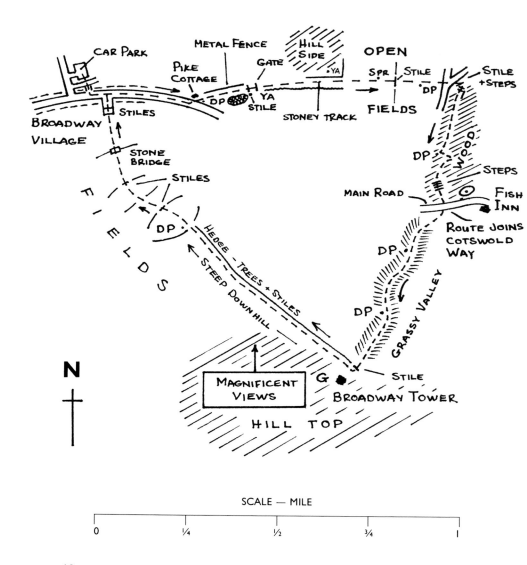

SCALE — MILE

| 0 | ¼ | ½ | ¾ | I |

grassy valleys, climbing at the end to arrive at the celebrated Broadway Tower. At 1,024 feet it is the second highest point of the Cotswolds, and from the top of the Tower twelve counties can be seen. On one fine day the writer observed the Malvern Hills, the Wrekin in Shropshire, the Clee Hills and even the Black Mountains of Wales.

G. Broadway Tower is a folly, built at the end of the eighteenth century to satisfy a whim of a countess. It has three round battlemented turrets with canted sides which, with its circular arches over the windows, give it a Saxon or Norman appearance. Curiously enough it is not built of local stone, for its architect, James Wyatt, considered the latter would not present the weather-matured finish he required. It is now part of the Broadway Tower Country Park, where large numbers of visitors enjoy the picnic area, the ancient Tower Barn, the nature walks and a museum.

Some famous people have been connected with Broadway and its celebrated tower, including William Morris, D. G. Rossetti and Edward Burne-Jones. The latter, noted as a pre-Raphaelite painter is said to have done some of his pictures up in the tower itself, whilst William Morris, social reformer, poet, painter and designer, is given credit as being the 'discoverer' of Broadway towards the end of the nineteenth century. In 1876 Morris wrote a letter from

Broadway Tower

13

the Tower which resulted in the formation of the Society for the Protection of Ancient Buildings.

There is now a two mile walk downhill back to the village which is so well marked that no detailed description is necessary. You will follow the hedge and trees for a mile until the path turns half left at a direction post. The way reaches the main road just above where you came through the alleyway from the car park.

Alternatives

1a   **4½ mile walk.** Circular route Broadway and Saintbury. (i.e. the first part of Walk 2)

1b   **4 miles.** Circular walk Broadway to Broadway Tower. (i.e. the second part of Walk 2)

1c   Walk to Broadway Tower and back. This can take in an hour or two of enjoyment at the Picnic Area. **Distance 4 miles.**

Parking

There is another excellent car park by the church at the bottom end of the village, with toilets, if this is more convenient for you.

WALK THREE

Stanton:
Circular Route

Distance: 6½ miles

The starting point for this walk is the car park at the entrance to the village. It is planned in an anti-clockwise direction in order to avoid the steep ascent to Shenberrow, but hardy walkers could, of course, do the route the other way round. If you plan it so that a mid-day lunch is required you will have to vary the way you go about it for the only inn available is the Mount up the hill in Stanton. In this case it is suggested that you begin at the entrance to Papermill Valley (B), which will enable you to reach Stanton by mid-day.

> **C.** The village of Stanton is one of the most delightful in the Cotswolds, with its single street normally uncluttered by cars (for there is no through road). Its lovely stone houses were built between 1570 and 1650 and the outstanding quality of their construction is due largely to the widespread restoration by Sir Philip Stott who bought the estate in 1906 and lived in the splendid Jacobean mansion — Stanton Court.
> The church, dating from late Norman to Perpendicular, has a charming spire. There are two pulpits, from one of which John Wesley preached one of his first sermons.

After leaving the car park (A) move off southwards, and where the road turns right follow the direction post which will set you on the delightful field pathway to Stanway, a mile-and-a-half away. This part of the walk is on the Cotswold Way long-distance path, and is well marked.

At the end of the field path, which passes through groups of magnificient oak, beech, ash and chestnut trees, you will reach the lane from Stanton. Turn left and pass round the front of the Manor House with its famous tithe barn. Just past the church is the celebrated three-storey gatehouse, said to be the work of Inigo Jones (D).

A few yards further on turn sharp left where a direction post indicates the way along an alley and across a sloping field, where the Cotswold Way

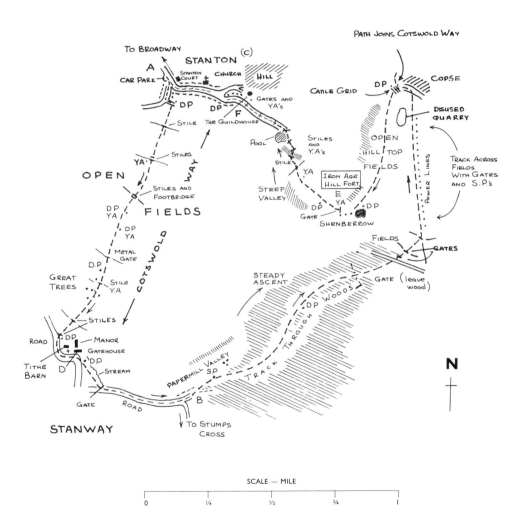

PATH JOINS COTSWOLD WAY

TO BROADWAY

STANTON (c)

A
CAR PARK
STANTON COURT
CHURCH
HILL

CATTLE GRID
DP
COPSE

DP   DP
GATES AND YA's

DISUSED QUARRY

STILE
THE GUILDHOUSE
F

POOL
STILES AND Y.A's

OPEN HILL TOP FIELDS

TRACK ACROSS FIELDS WITH GATES AND S.P.'s

YA
STILES

STILE
Y.A

OPEN
WAY

STILES AND FOOTBRIDGE

STEEP VALLEY

IRON AGE HILL FORT
E
YA

POWER LINES

FIELDS

DP
YA

FIELDS

DP
GATE
SHENBERROW

GATES

DP
YA

COTSWOLD

METAL GATE

D.P.

GREAT TREES

STILE Y.A

STEADY ASCENT

GATE (LEAVE WOOD)

DP WOODS

STILES

ROAD
DP
MANOR GATEHOUSE

TITHE BARN
D
DP
STREAM

PAPERMILL VALLEY
SP

TRACK THROUGH

N

GATE
ROAD

B

STANWAY

TO STUMPS CROSS

SCALE — MILE

0   ¼   ½   ¾   1

leaves you on its way to Wood Stanton.

Follow the road until it turns sharp right to Stumps Cross. Here you turn left onto a track which for three quarters of a mile leads you on a gradual ascent through Longpark and Lidicombe woods in a north-easterly direction. The first part passes the beautiful Papermill Valley, where the writer once saw a kestrel. In summer these woods are very attractive indeed.

At the top of the long rise you come out of the wood, walk a short way along a track then come out into open fields. Two of these are crossed in a north-easterly direction when you veer left onto a long straight track, heading due north. After more than half a mile a narrow lane crosses the track. Turn left here and almost immediately there is a junction where the Cotswold Way joins our walk. Turn left over the cattle grid and proceed in a southerly direction across open hilltop fields.

In about half a mile the path reaches the settlement of Shenberrow, with its farm and tiny cluster of houses. This was once an Iron-age hill-fort, the remains of whose ramparts can still be discerned.

E. Shenberrow hill-fort was one of seventeen Iron-age hill-forts that have been located along the Cotswold escarpment, having been constructed c. 6/800 B.C. This bivellate hill-fort (one with two surrounding ramparts)

The Cotswold Way — across the fields to Stanway

17

The village of Stanton

originally covered 4½ acres. During brief excavations in 1935 some pottery, bone needles, a bronze bracelet and an iron knife were found there.

Pass through an iron gate, go straight over (do not turn right) and plunge down into a steep valley, which is clearly marked. Signs will guide you all the way to the bottom, where you will come to a number of stiles. Go to the eastern side of a small reservoir and then onto a track, where you turn left.

After a third of a mile you enter Stanton at the opposite end to where you started.

It is to be hoped that you can spare the time to look at the lovely houses, pay a visit to the church and, if possible, go and see the Guildhouse at the top end of the village (near the Mount).

F. The quiet beauty of the village of Stanton has been enriched over recent years by a new centre of creative living in the form of a Guildhouse, which was built between 1963 and 1973.

This enterprise owes its existence to the selfless labours of devoted volunteers, motivated by the lifelong ambition of Mary Osborn. The erection of a truly splendid building is in the best traditions of Cotswold stone architecture. It stands high on the hillside, and can cater for sizeable groups including accommodation for up to ten students who come on courses.

The Guildhouse, which is interdenominational, offers friendship and facilities for the practice of rural crafts — spinning, dyeing, weaving, caligraphy, woodwork, pottery, art, etc.

Alternatives

1a If you take sandwiches and are not relying on buying a mid-day meal you could start at Stanway or the entrance to Papermill Valley, and do the whole circular walk.

1b **3 miles.** A delightful walk across fields from Stanton to Stanway and back.

Parking

There is an official car park at the entrance to Stanton (marked A on the map). Cars can be parked on the roadside at Stanway and the entrance to Papermill Valley.

WALK FOUR

Cleeve Hill to Hailes Abbey

Distance: 8½ miles

This is one of the few walks in the book that is not circular, so you will need two cars — one at each end of the route. Car parking is not easy at the starting point, there being only one small park some 400 yards from the entrance to the common, and that is often full. The Rising Sun Hotel, which has a large car park have always been obliging to the writer and may be for you. (A).

There is an exit at the top right hand corner of the Hotel car park which leads one onto the Common. There you will immediately see a multi-arm direction post, which may tend to confuse you, but for this walk you go in a north-easterly direction straight up the hillside (which is very steep). If you continued on it would lead you to the Topographical Point, but for Walk Four you turn left (north) round the side of the hill. You are now on the Cotswold Way, which you will follow all the way to Hailes Abbey.

The Cotswold Way path used to go the other way round the Common, but was re-routed some time ago. You might prefer the southerly way which is shorter and easier. If so once you have climbed on to the top of the escarpment you will (weather permitting) see the three Masts in the distance. Make for these, where shortly after you will link with the authentic Cotswold Way. (B)

The way on the Common is well marked past the Golf Club House, the stone wall round the end of the Postlip complex, the Washpool and the final section through gorse and heather. The map is explicit enough.

The end of the Common is reached at a gate, after which two fields lead to Wontleys Farm, where you turn sharp left onto a track. Continue north-eastwards for about half-a-mile when the way turns right at a direction post.

Cross a large field keeping to the right of the wall and you will come to a very famous Ancient Monument (C).

C. When Belas Knap was constructed there was no such place as London

20

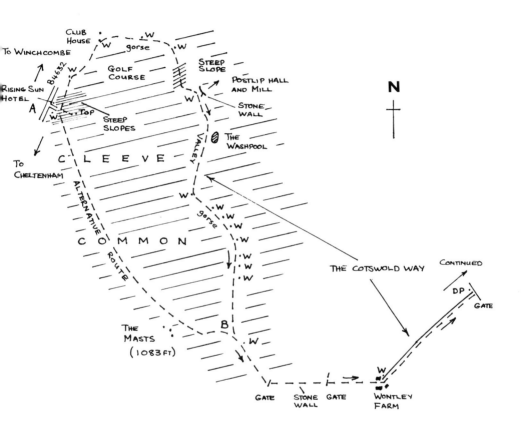

To Winchcombe

CLUB HOUSE

B4632

RISING SUN HOTEL

A

W Top

STEEP SLOPES

GOLF COURSE

gorse

W

W

STEEP SLOPE

POSTLIP HALL AND MILL

STONE WALL

VALLEY

THE WASHPOOL

To CHELTENHAM

C L E E V E

ALTERNATIVE ROUTE

C O M M O N

gorse

W
W
W
W
W
W

N

THE COTSWOLD WAY

CONTINUED

DP

GATE

THE MASTS (1083 FT)

B

W

GATE   STONE WALL   GATE

W

WONTLEY FARM

SCALE — MILE

0   ¼   ½   ¾   1

21

no Parthenon stood over the Acropolis in ancient Greece and civilisation was only emerging in Egypt. This neolithic monument is probably five thousand years old — i.e. it was three thousand years old when the Romans were at Wadfield, just down the hill. The great long barrow is 178 feet long by 60 feet wide, and is built of oolitic slabs and walling stones.

Excavations were made in 1863/5 and 1928/30, and the remains of thirty eight people were found, and behind the false entrance in the north end were discovered the skull of a man and bones of five children.

Turn immediately sharp left, then right and follow the path down to a lane the other side a small copse. Turn right and follow the lane for about a quarter of a mile, then go left past Humblebee Cottages down a track to Wadfield Farm.

There now follows a most pleasant walk over six fields, towards the end of which you will see Sudeley Castle over to your right (D).

D. Sudeley Castle, equally with the old Abbey of Winchcombe (long since destroyed) has played a major part in the history of the town. The original castle was built in the reign of Stephen, but its time of eminence came during the rule of Henry VIII, when Anne Boleyn, Catherine of Aragon and Elizabeth all stayed there. After the death of the King in 1547 his wife and last Queen,

A view of Cleeve Common

Belas Knap — neolithic long barrow

Catherine Parr, had secretly married Baron Seymour, and it was at Sudeley Castle that this accomplished woman spent the last short months of her life. She is buried in the Castle church.

The Castle was badly damaged in the Civil War, but was restored in the nineteenth century. During recent times Emma Dent made its return to some of its former glory her life's work. It holds many antiques and treasures, and is open to the public during the summer months.

Walk up the lane, over the River Isbourne, and enter Winchcombe which is probably the oldest place in the Cotswolds.

The great church stands opposite to you as you reach the main road which runs through the centre of the small town.

E. The Parish Church of St. Peter, Winchcombe, which stands on the site of an earlier church, dates from 1470 and is a true Cotswold 'wool' church. It is built by the side of where the Benedictine Abbey stood before its destruction. It is Perpendicular in style, spacious and lofty, with a beautiful carved rood-screen. Arthur Mee described the fifteenth century clerestory as one of the finest in England. The church was restored in 1873.

The altar cloth, hanging in a frame by the north door, was made from a

WALK FOUR

(PART B)

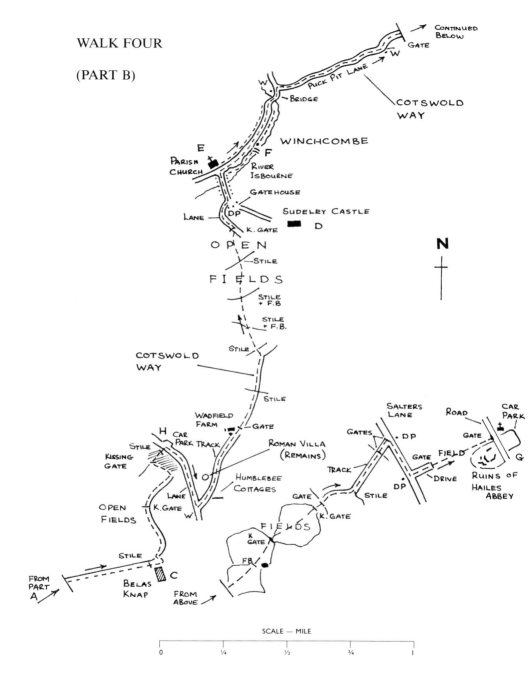

CONTINUED BELOW

GATE

W

PUCK PIT LANE

W

BRIDGE

COTSWOLD WAY

WINCHCOMBE

E

PARISH CHURCH

F

RIVER ISBOURNE

GATEHOUSE

SUDELEY CASTLE

LANE

DP

D

K. GATE

O P E N

STILE

F I E L D S

STILE + F.B

STILE + F.B.

COTSWOLD WAY

STILE

STILE

N

WADFIELD FARM

GATE

H

CAR PARK TRACK

ROMAN VILLA (REMAINS)

SALTERS LANE

ROAD

CAR PARK

GATES

DP

GATE

FIELD

STILE

KISSING GATE

O

HUMBLEBEE COTTAGES

TRACK

GATE

DRIVE

G

RUINS OF HAILES ABBEY

LANE

K. GATE

W

GATE

STILE

DP

OPEN FIELDS

F I E L D S

K. GATE

K GATE

STILE

FB

FROM PART A

C

BELAS KNAP

FROM ABOVE

SCALE — MILE

0   ¼   ½   ¾   1

priest's cope of the fourteenth century. Queen Catherine of Aragon, while staying at Sudeley Castle, added the surrounding border with her own pomegranate badge.

Stone coffins are thought to be those of St Kenelm and King Kenulf. The church is renowned for the forty grotesque gargoyles in its stone walls.

For those who have done the first six miles of the walk in one go the thought of a snack lunch will be attractive. There are inns and restaurants along the High Street to the right where the route now proceeds. Half way along once stood the George Inn, but alas this famous spot has now been converted into living quarters.

F. The George Inn had stood on this site for seven hundred years, and had a long association with pilgrims visiting Hailes Abbey. In the yard at the side there could be seen a great stone bath, known as the 'Monk's Bath', where one could imagine the returning pilgrims at their ablutions!

The last two and a half miles of this walk lies along the Pilgrims Way used by the monks.

Continue along the High Street and cross the bridge over the river Isbourne at the bottom. After a short distance you will see a waymark directing you right up Puck Pit Lane. This lane, which can be muddy in wet weather, goes for half a mile until a gate leads into fields. The route continues in a north-easterly direction, well-marked, until one reaches a track which after some four hundred yards, leads into a minor road called Salters' Lane.

Turn sharp right and then left after two hundred yards. The crossing of a field now leads you to the end of the walk at Hailes Abbey.

G. The Abbey of Hailes was one of the last Cistercian houses to be raised in England, and its remote position in a woodland setting at the foot of the Cotswold Hills was ideal for its austere form of religious life. It was founded in 1245 under a grant from Henry III, with twenty monks and ten lay brothers.

In the year 1270 a phial of Holy Blood was presented to the Community by the Patriarch of Jerusalem, later to become Pope Urban IV, and this attracted great crowds as one of the pilgrim centres of England.

The Abbey was destroyed at the Dissolution in 1558.

Alternatives

1a The walk can be done in reverse, but the steady climb from Winchcombe to Belas Knap and the final section on Cleeve

Common (the highest part of the Cotswolds) makes the route more arduous this way round.

1b It is a pleasant walk of about **5 miles** to start at Hailes Abbey, undertake the Pilgrims Way to Winchcombe and return the same way.

1c **2 miles.** Walk to Belas Knap. A side road from Winchcombe will take you to the monument car park (H) from which you ascend across fields to the neolithic barrow.

1d **4 miles.** Especially on a nice day it is a delightful outing to walk round the perimeter of Cleeve Common using the Cotswold Way route outgoing and returning by the alternative way shown on the map.

Parking

Easy at Hailes Abbey but difficult at Cleeve Common. Please see comments at the beginning of the script for this walk. If you want to use Winchcombe there is a car park opposite the church and another off the High Street to the north-west.

Bourton-on-the-Water Circular Route

Distance: 6½ miles

Bourton-on-the-Water has been described as not only one of the prettiest villages in England but also 'the Venice of the Cotswolds'. This expresses the effect produced by the wide section of the river Windrush flowing alongside the village High Street, enhanced by the green verges and the charming low stone bridges, without parapets, which cross the river. The extensive open village centre has an attraction of its own, but there are other features which make Bourton one of the most popular places in the Cotswolds.

A. One of the big draws is Birdland. This magnificent bird sanctuary is built on 3½ acres of land in the Curator's sixteenth century residence, and has some six hundred different species, including many tropical varieties. There are seven types of penguin, one of the finest collections in Europe, in a pool where you can see them swimming underwater. There are also flamingoes and gaudy parrots who will talk to you if you persist.

B. Another famous feature is the Model Village. The united efforts of seven people completed the construction in four years. It is an exact replica of Bourton-on-the-Water to a one-ninth scale. It has a live running river and even a model of the model.

Car parking is explained at the end of this walk, but if you can find a spot along the side of the High Street it will be convenient.

Walk to the bottom of the street (south-eastwards) and turn left opposite the post office into Station Road. You will pass the Baptist church on the left. About 150 yards ahead where there is a garage turn right at a direction post and follow the path. After a short distance bear left and then go through a bar gate onto a metalled road, where you turn right.

Continue along the track in a south-easterly direction for 500 yards, then turn left at a direction on a telegraph post. To your right you will see an

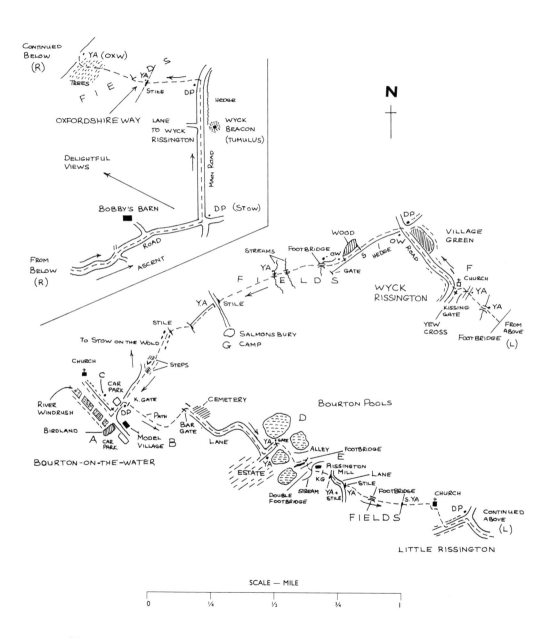

CONTINUED
BELOW
(R)

YA (OXW)

TREES

F I E L D S

YA

STILE

DP

HEDGE

OXFORDSHIRE WAY

LANE
TO WYCK
RISSINGTON

WYCK
BEACON
(TUMULUS)

DELIGHTFUL
VIEWS

MAIN ROAD

N

BOBBY'S BARN

DP (STOW)

FROM
BELOW
(R)

ROAD

ASCENT

STREAMS

FOOTBRIDGE

WOOD

OW

S HEDGE

OW ROAD

DP

VILLAGE
GREEN

YA

F I E L D S

GATE

WYCK
RISSINGTON

F

CHURCH

YA

YA

KISSING
GATE

YA.A

STILE

STILE

SALMONSBURY
CAMP

G

YEW
CROSS

FOOTBRIDGE

FROM
ABOVE
(L)

To STOW ON THE WOLD

STEPS

CHURCH

C

CAR
PARK

RIVER
WINDRUSH

K. GATE

CEMETERY

BOURTON POOLS

D

BIRDLAND

DP

PATH

A

CAR
PARK

MODEL
VILLAGE

B

BAR
GATE

LANE

YA

GATE

ALLEY

FOOTBRIDGE

E

BOURTON-ON-THE-WATER

ESTATE

YA

RISSINGTON
MILL

KG

LANE

STILE

FOOTBRIDGE

CHURCH

DOUBLE
FOOTBRIDGE

STREAM

YA +
STILE

YA

S. YA

DP.

CONTINUED
ABOVE
(L)

F I E L D S

LITTLE RISSINGTON

SCALE — MILE

0   ¼   ½   ¾   1

estate of houses. In 80 yards pass through a gate, and here you reach the Bourton Pools.

D. The Pools or Quarry Lakes have been artificially created out of old gravel pits. The idea is to create nature reserves with swans, mallard, moorhens and other wildfowl. In due course they will become an attractive inducement to come to Bourton-on-the-Water.

Follow the yellow arrow signs until you reach Rissington Mill (E) by passing over a double footbridge spanning the stream. This was an old corn mill whose unused wheel is still extant.

Continue ahead for a short way then strike to the left over three fields where the lane goes to the right. A modest climb will bring you to Little Risssington Church whose grounds you enter through a kissing gate. The church has an Early English chancel and there are many Royal Air Force graves in the cemetery.

Leave the churchyard by the south gate and cross one field to enter the village of Little Rissington. Follow the road round to the left and ignore the direction post on the corner. Continue uphill in a north-easterly bearing for more than half-a-mile, passing Bobby's Barn en route.

Turn left when you reach the main road (signposted to Stow) and continue northwards for about threequarters of a mile. This road section is unavoidable as there is no public right of way across the fields, but it is quite acceptable as a pleasant grass path goes alongside the road. About half way along on the right is the Wyck Beacon Tumulus with its copse of trees which are typical of an ancient burial ground.

Where the road commences to turn right take a field path to the left where there is a direction post. This is part of the Oxfordshire Way — but, alas —there was no sign at this point, when we passed, to indicate so. The way is clearly marked except at the end of the second long sloping field which is confusing when you reach the trees. Bear slightly right at the end of this large field — you won't go far wrong if you keep going westwards.

This field path will lead you to Wyck Rissington church.

F. The Church of St Lawrence is quite fascinating, the leaflet about it being full of interesting reading. Its architecture covers six hundred years, its thirteenth century chancel being its main glory.

Gustav Holst was organist here as a young man, living in a cottage on the green. The East Window has been described as one of the gems of the Cotswolds. The reredos is a memorial to a parishioner who won the V.C.

Facing the road in the churchyard is a famous feature — 'The Living Cross'. It is shaped from a yew tree and is nine feet high.

A very large old stone vicarage stands to the side of the church. It was once famous because it had a maze in the grounds. A massive Wellington pine stands where was the centre of the maze. It was planted by the grandfather of Archbishop Fisher.

Continue through the village to the end of the Green, where you will see an unusual row of staddle stones. Our walk now goes to the left across fields all the way back to Bourton. You will be moving in a south-westerly direction. Two words of caution — when you have passed the small wood on the right do not go through the gate ahead but bear round to the right (it is marked) and when you come to the track which goes left to Salmonsbury Camp the yellow arrow ahead over the stile seems to point left across the next field. In fact, keep right by the hedge.

G. Salmonsbury Camp is not now very impressive, having been partially destroyed by ploughing. It was made in the Iron Age and covered fifty-six acres. Various remains have been discovered in different excavations — sites of circular huts, currency bars and two crouched inhumation burials.

At the end of the field path turn left and follow the road into the High Street — where you started.

The Village of Bourton-on-the-Water

C. A further attraction you should not miss is the superb model railway laid out in shop premises half way up the High Street on the right hand side. Twenty trains run through scenery varying from snow-covered mountains to model towns. One of its joys is that part of the layout can be operated by visitors.

Alternatives

1a **2 miles.** A short walk from Bourton-on-the-Water to Rissington Mill and back.

1b **5 miles.** Parking your car on the village green at Wyck Rissington it is a lovely walk on a summer's day to walk to Bourton-on-the-Water and back. Refreshments are obtainable in Bourton.

1c **2 miles.** Using two cars make it a single route to walk from Bourton-on-the-Water to Little Rissington.

Parking:

The most convenient, if you can find a space, is along the right hand side of the High Street. There are two other parks — (1) along Station Road next to the garage and (2) just beyond the Model Village on the other side of the road.

WALK SIX

Lower Slaughter: Circular Route via Naunton

Distance: 9 miles

This is certainly one of the loveliest walks in the Cotswolds, much of it along the Windrush Valley and the rest over delightful green fields and through pleasant woods. What climbing is involved is very easy.

The two Slaughter villages are renowned and attract large numbers of visitors. Lower Slaughter, where the walk starts, has no car park so motorists use the side of the road at the entrance to this delightful place where the river Eye flows through the centre of the village, giving it a mildly Venetian atmosphere.

Walk alongside the small river past typical Cotswold stone cottages, and where you turn right, on the opposite side, is a picturesque corn mill wheel.

A. The Slaughters do not derive their name from demise of cattle, but from the De Sclotre family, who owned land in Norman times.

Lower Slaughter openly admits it has nothing to offer but peace and beauty, but these two qualities are sufficient to draw hordes of visitors. The village is certainly quaint with its tiny bridges over the river and the mill wheel at the end.

The church of St. Mary's dating from the thirteenth century, became unsafe and had to be rebuilt in 1866. Besides the beautiful spire the outstanding feature is the alabaster reredos.

The walk starts at the post office where you turn left at the direction marked 'Warden's Way'. Proceed north-westwards for three quarters of a mile across green fields to Upper Slaughter.

Turn left at the road and pass the entrance to the Lords of the Manor Hotel. This great mansion used to be the vicarage, so you can imagine what a wealthy man the incumbent was (B).

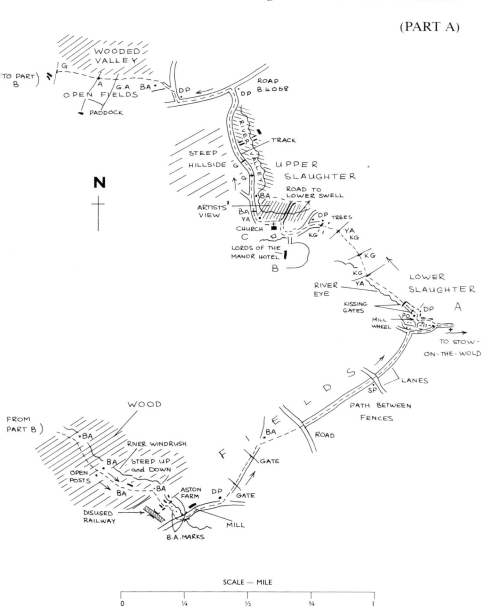

SCALE — MILE

0   ¼   ½   ¾   1

C. St Peter's Church was originally Norman but it was restored in 1877. There is a mortuary chapel to a former vicar who was Lord of the Manor.

Pass to the right of the church and in fifty yards a gorgeous miniature view will enchant your eyes as you look down on the small river, the footbridge, ford and cluster of houses. It is a celebrated spot where one can often see groups of artists intent on painting the vista before them.

Take the track behind the church, walking northwards with the river valley down below you on the right. In less than a mile you will reach the B 4068 road. Go left and follow the road for about 350 yards when the route goes right at a direction post. Take the lefthand path which goes immediately past a row of terraced cottages up over open fields with a wooded valley to your right. The way now lies westwards.

It is easy to lose your way over these large fields. Keep well to the right of the fencing round a paddock and buildings away to your left. The route is well marked and will shortly bring you down to a road. Turn right here and proceed for about one hundred yards when you will bear left at a signpost pointing to Guiting Power and Winchcombe along the road you are leaving.

The path is now in the fields, running along side the lane, and as there is a sign 'beware of the bull' I shall hardly blame you if you stick to the lane.

The Village of Lower Slaughter

The lovely Windrush Valley

In a quarter of a mile turn left onto a track (southwards) and follow the signs to Naunton. If you turn left and then left again it will bring you to the Black Horse Inn.

D. The village of Naunton is attractively sited in a small valley, and mainly consists of a single street. Its two chief features are the other end from the Inn, but you might care to walk up to see the church and dovecote, especially if you are only doing half the walk.

According to David Verey St Andrew's parish church is a Perpendicular 'wool' church. Its greatest treasure is the stone carved fifteenth century pulpit, which is richly decorated with canopy panels, pinnacled buttresses and tracery. The font is also fifteenth century.

The famous dovecote, by the river, is seventeenth century, and has four high gables with a central turret and four-centred arch doorway. It has over a thousand nest holes.

For the second part of the walk bear half right from the Inn and follow the track due south (there are no markers) which goes uphill until you reach the road (B.4068). Turn right and almost immediately left at a direction post then move southwards until you strike the river. The next

WALK SIX

(PART B)

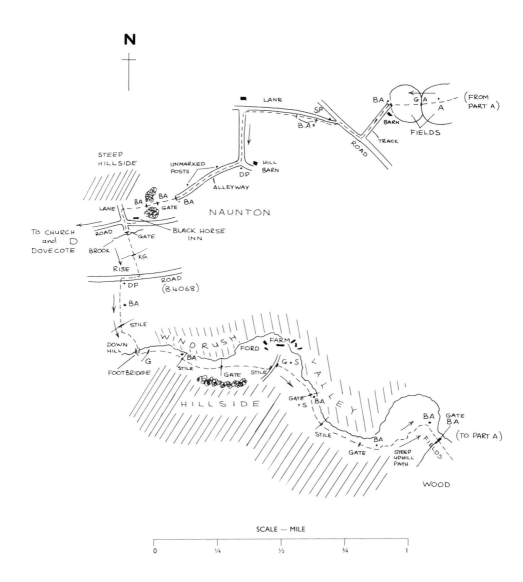

two miles are in the beautiful Windrush Valley and require little description as the way is well marked.

The latter part of the valley path lies through a wood and you will eventually come to Aston Farm where you turn left on the road down to the bridge over the river. The lane goes past a Mill and merges into a track where your path bears left at a direction post. You will now be heading north-east passing two gates before bearing right at a blue arrow sign.

The rest of the way lies over fields, crossing a road and a lane before leading back into the village of Lower Slaughter.

Alternatives

1a   **4½ miles.** With two cars you can do half the main walk from Lower Slaughter to Naunton.

1b   **4½ miles.** Again requiring two cars, the second half of the main route along the delightful Windrush Valley from Naunton to Lower Slaughter.

1c   **2 miles.** From Lower Slaughter across the fields to Upper Slaughter and back. A most pleasant afternoon's ramble.

Parking

No parking in Lower Slaughter except alongside the road leading to the village. Can be difficult during the summer season.

In Naunton there is parking at the Black Horse Inn at the eastern end of the village. At the other end there are places where you can park.

Cheltenham: Circular Route via Coberley

Distance: 7 miles

This walk starts on the south side of Cheltenham where the Leckhampton Road (B.4070) joins the Old Bath Road. There is a very convenient bus stop here if you are not using a car. If you are it can be parked at this corner on the Old Bath Road.

Proceed up Birdlip road for about 50 yards then turn left along Undercliff Avenue. At the end the road becomes a track, along which you shortly encounter a stile, then bear right into a large field which slopes upwards towards the hills. There are bushes to your right and then left past which continue to the top, where two stiles lead into Daisy Bank Road.

Go straight over, then follow the track for some 500 yards up a rather arduous ascent, passing at the top two small stone ruins. The path now levels out and you will shortly reach the famous Devil's Chimney. It lies on your right but as a mound stands in front you will have to go past it to get a good view.

> **A.** The Devil's Chimney is a remarkably formed pinnacle of limestone rock that at some period in history became detached from the precipitous rock face.
>
> It has been said that it is rather perilously perched and at some time may crash to the ground, but it looks solid enough at the present.

In a short distance you will join the Cotswold Way coming round from Charlton Kings Common. After about 500 yards you will pass a disused quarry on the right and reach a road. Turn left and proceed in a north-easterly direction for 200 yards.

This is slightly uphill, at the end of which the Cotswold Way turns sharp right where there is a direction post. Continue straight on along the lane until you come to Hartley's Farm when the path goes right alongside a stone wall. Shortly you will pass over a stile and move down into the valley called Hartley Bottom.

Pass the old pump house and after 250 yards with the wood on the left

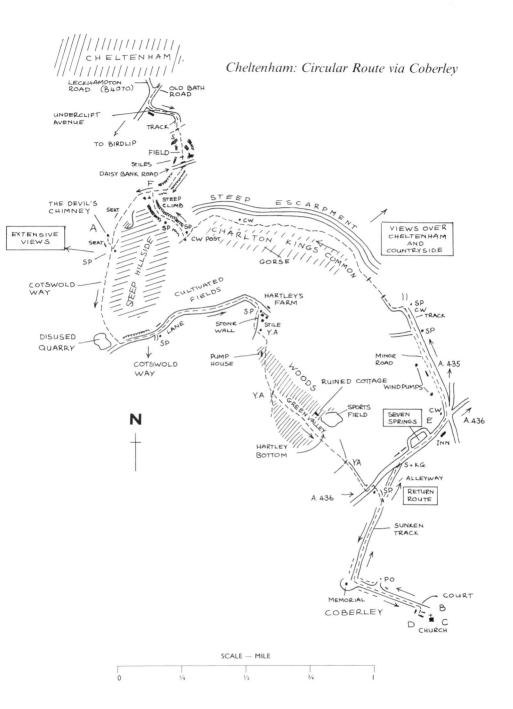

Cheltenham: Circular Route via Coberley

you will reach a point where the paths divide. Go over the stile to take the lefthand route down through a delightful green valley moving down through the woods. When you get to the end of the trees you will see a ruined cottage to your left in the wood, and beyond it a sports field. Go over a stile in the far left corner of the field and follow the hedge to the A.436 road.

In the early summer there were to be seen a profusion of campion and forget-me-nots on the side of the path. Turn left, then after 10 yards right onto a bridle path, signposted 'Coberley 0.5 k'. Follow the hedge on the left for 350 yards, when the path becomes a sunken lane leading into the village of Coberley.

The return route retraces your steps for a short way from the Cross where you will now be standing, but it is recommended that you go along a short distance to see Coberley Court.

B. Coberley is associated with the Berkeley family, the wealthy land owners who possessed about half of Gloucestershire in the twelfth century.

The present Coberley Court may disappoint you for as you pass through its

The green valley of Hartley Bottom

Where Dick Whittington was born

central archway it may appear not much more than a large farm, but you should persist to the church beyond.

C. The Church of St. Giles is quite magnificent and beautifully maintained. It has some fine stained-glass windows. There are two tombs in the side chapel: (1) of Sir Thomas Berkeley, who fought at the Battle of Crecy, and built the South Chapel c. 1340 and (2) of his wife Lady Joan Berkeley, who afterwards married Sir William Whittington and was the mother of Dick Whittington, who thrice became Lord Mayor of London.

D. On the south side of the church there is a boundary wall which is all that remains of the original Manor House where Dick Whittington lived as a boy. The wall is pierced by two Elizabethan doorways, the larger one being opposite the door into the South Chapel, whilst the smaller one is blocked up.

Return past the post office to the Cross and walk north-eastwards along the sunken track on which you came into Coberley. Where it turns left there is a signpost to Seven Springs where you will follow the alleyway to the A.436 road. A short distance along to the right is Seven Springs.

E. Some people assert that Seven Springs is, in fact, the source of the Thames, because this tributary rises furthest from the mouth of the great river, in the wall built on the roadside where the springs gush into the hollow — as if to make an attestation of this claim for Old Father Thames.

There is a plaque bearing the inscription:

'Hic tuus — O Tamesine pater,
Septemgeminus fons.'

Nevertheless, it is traditionally accepted that the real source of the Thames is at Thames Head, three miles south-west of Cirencester near the village of Coates.

Follow round to the big road junction, bearing left at the metalled lane going in a north-westerly direction. There is a signpost showing that we are again on the Cotswold Way, and shall continue thereon for the next two miles. The lane passes Windmill Farm and after half-a-mile turns left, but you will go straight on along a track.

In two hundred yards the route goes left and starts a steady climb up onto Charlton Kings Common on which a delightful path wends its way through gorse bushes and provides magnificent views over Cheltenham and the countryside.

The walk over this lovely part of the Cotswold Hills goes for about a mile when it begins to turn south-west. Just before you reach the Beacon a stone direction marker points sharp right 'footpath to Leckhampton Hill', which will lead you through the woods downhill to join the outward route not far from where the walk started (F).

Alternatives

1a **2 mile walk** to the Devil's Chimney and back. Quite a climb to start with but well worth the effort to see the remarkable rock formation, and the views.

1b With two cars you can walk from Hartley Farm to Coberley (**about 2 miles**) through the lovely Hartley Bottom valley.

1c **2 miles.** From Coberley to Seven Springs and back. An interesting short walk.

1d **4 miles.** Parking your car at Seven Springs, walk up onto Charlton Kings Common and back. In the sunshine this is magnificent.

Parking

Cars can be parked in Old Bath Road for this main walk. There is provided car parking at Seven Springs, and places can be found in the village of Coberley.

Bibury: Circular Walk

Distance: 8½ miles

This is a lovely walk, especially the second half along the river Coln and there is very little climbing.

It starts near the church in Bibury, with car parking along the road by the side of the river.

> **A.** It is certain that there was a Saxon church in this site, but in 1130 it passed to the Abbey of Osney near Oxford. In this Norman period the nave was lengthened and aisles added. In the fifteenth century the Early English tower was raised to complete the church as we know it today.
>
> The exterior presents a lovely picture with its tidy churchyard adorned by paths lined with standard roses. Bale tombs attest to the influence of the wool trade.
>
> The interior has much of interest, fully described in the local booklet. Notice the remarkable Saxon jambs supporting the chancel arch, the 700-year-old square font, the eight aumbries and the quaint 1927 glass window depicting Mr Cooper's coach from Bibury Court, still remembered by aged locals.
>
> In three hundred years Bibury Parish Church has had only ten vicars — which speaks for itself!

After 80 yards turn left over the river bridge and almost immediately view the famous Arlington Row.

> **B.** Arlington Row comprises a very old line of Cotswold cottages. It was built in the late fourteenth century as a wool store, but it was converted into weavers' cottages in the seventeenth century. It is now owned by the National Trust.

Continue uphill past Rosemary Cottage, bear left at the signpost and in forty yards a gate leads into fields. There is a direction post with five signs on it. You go straight ahead. Continue for about 350 years with a hedge

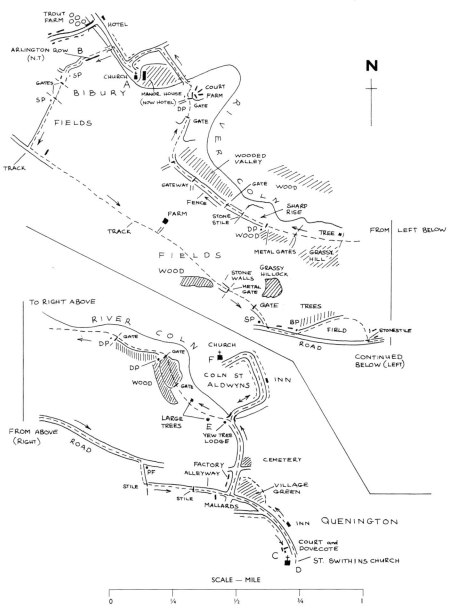

N

SCALE — MILE

0   ¼   ½   ¾   1

on it. You go straight ahead. Continue for about 350 yards with a hedge on your right until you come to a track where you turn sharp left. You will now be going south-east with a stone wall on your right. There is no direction marker at this corner.

You will follow this track in a south-easterly direction for another mile-and-a-half until you reach a road, which is, in fact, the Roman Road — Akeman Street. Turn left along this road and just past two houses on the left a sign post directs you across a large field. Move in a semi-circle to come out on the same road by a farm house. Follow the road eastwards for a third of a mile.

Leave the road to the right at a signpost marked 'public footpath' and after 200 yards turn left over a stile to walk along the lefthand hedge of a large field. You will then cross another stile into an alleyway which leads past a house called "Mallards" when the route enters Quenington.

There is a large village green at the top, and it is worth walking down to the bottom to see Quenington Court and its famous dovecote (C) and the church.

D. The fame of St Swithin's church reposes in the two Norman doorways,

Arlington Row — Bibury

The valley of the Coln

which should be accorded more than a casual glance, for the wealth of their carving is worth study. There is a superb tympanum over the north doorway whose subject, the Harrowing of Hell, shows Christ triumphant over Sin and Death.

There is an inn half way up the village street, but you might prefer to go on another mile to take refreshment in Coln St. Aldwyns. You now go back to the top of the village green and turn right onto the road which passes a factory and then plunges down a short hill to cross the river Coln and enter Coln St. Aldwyns.

Take the road along the riverside, pass the old mill and you will see the inn on your right. If you wish to see the church continue to the top of the village.

F. The church has an impressive tower with four golden crocketed pinnacles, and a fine Norman doorway. John Keble's father was vicar here for many years and his son, founder of the Oxford Movement, was his curate for a time.

The nearby manor house was the home of Sir Michael Hicks-Beach, one-time Chancellor of the Exchequer.

Now retrace your steps to the river bridge (E) where the delightful second half of the walk starts, along the Coln valley. The route is easy to follow because the path keeps close to the river all the way back to Bibury.

The path becomes a track towards the end, where it passes Court Farm and once more crosses the river bridge. The view to the left is a well-known photographer's dream with the old manor house (now a hotel) providing a picturesque backcloth. Follow the road straight ahead and turn left at the top to bring you back to the starting point.

Alternatives

1a The walk can be reduced to about **7 miles** by cutting out the exploration of Quenington and Coln St. Aldwyns.

1b Motor to Coln St. Aldwyns and park the car near the river bridge along the road. Walk along the Coln to Bibury and back — a distance of about **4 miles**. There is a teashop just beyond the church at Bibury where you can refresh yourself.

1c **2 miles.** A relaxed walk along the river Coln either way if you have two cars.

Parking

At Bibury — along the roadside between the church and the river bridge.
At Coln St. Aldwyns — On the road along the riverside.

WALK NINE

Painswick: Circular Route

Distance: 6 miles

There is a convenient car park, with toilets, just south of the church for this attractive walk.

As you go out turn right and after 80/90 yards right again through the lychgate into the churchyard, where you will be astonished to see so many yew trees.

> **A.** The churchyard is one of the most unique in England, with two principal glories.
>
> First, the beautifully maintained yew trees, of which (though I made no attempt to count them) there are said to be 99. Any local inhabitant will tell you that it has always proved impossible to grow the hundredth! Some of them are over two hundred years old.
>
> Secondly, the numerous table tombs, which can have no equal. These lavish memorials to the dead were mainly the work of a talented local carver, John Bryan (d.1787) and his two sons. The skillful Renaissance designs are shown to their best amidst the yews.
>
> Once a year, on the 19th September, or the first Sunday thereafter, there is an annual Clipping Service where the clergy, choir and three hundred children encircle the church with an unbroken chain of hands. This is known as 'embracing the church'.

Just to the left as you leave the churchyard are the stocks, which are one of only two known iron stocks. They were placed there in the early seventeenth century, near to the Court House where the constable lived.

As you move past the street known as the Cross and into Bisley Street you will see facing you the fine Painswick Institute Club of which the town is proud.

On the left you will come to a row of weavers' cottages, indicative of the days of prosperity. Indeed, by 1800 there were over twenty cloth mills operating, some remains of which we shall see on the walk.

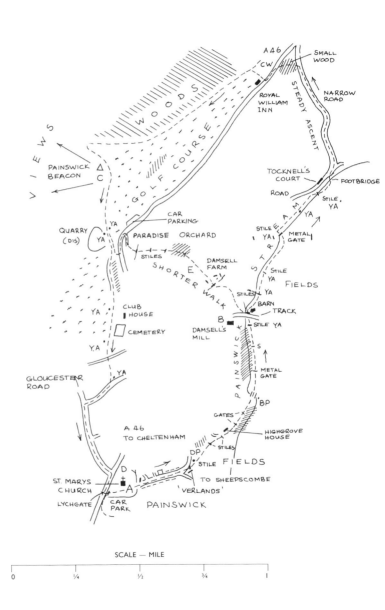

SCALE — MILE

0	¼	½	¾	1

After the turn to Sheepscombe, and just beyond the house called 'Verlands', turn right over a stile and go down the field towards the trees. Cross the stream, and after the next meadow join the grassy bridle path from the left. After passing two gates you cross the stream and are now on it's right. For the next 400 yards follow the path between a fence and tree-lined stream on your left. A stile with yellow arrows leads you out to Damsell's Mill.

> **B.** The mill is now privately owned, and if you want to see the huge old water wheel you have to obtain permission from the owner — for it is *inside* the house.
>
> It is amazing to find this old relic is made of metal, except for the wooden struts, and is no less than fourteen feet in diameter. It is still in situ where it operated the power when Damsell's was a corn and cloth mill in turn. It is three hundred years old. The water was stored in a small reservoir across the road, from where it flowed under the house.

The short walk goes left from here (see description later). The main route goes to the left of a small barn and right of the stream. There are fields on

Damsell's Mill

51

Painswick valley walk

your right, but keep near the stream which you cross over after some 400 yards. Now on the left of the water cross a large field to reach Tocknell's Court, a minor road coming in from the left.

Yellow arrows now direct you to the right of the stream for about 80 yards when you cross a wooden footbridge on to the road.

To reach the second half of this walk one now has about half-a-mile uphill on a narrow road. Towards the top when you can see the sign post at the main road turn left on a short track through a wood (there is no direction marker). Diagonally to your left you will see the Royal William Inn, where food and drink are available.

A drive on the north side of the inn will link you with the Cotswold Way. Turn left and follow the path across the golf course for about a mile alongside the woods. A short, sharp climb brings one to the highest point — Painswick Beacon.

C. It wasn't until the Saxons came that a small 'wicke' (a village) was established where Painswick church now stands. In Celtic and Roman times the Kimsbury Camp on the site where the Beacon now is was the habitation centre. It was ideal for defence — looking down to the west and eastwards. The double rampart can still be discerned, though there has been damage from time to time.

Cross the golf course, moving due south until you reach the lower path going parallel to the Cotswold Way. You will see a yellow arrow down a track to the left – this is the top end of the short walk. You continue past the quarry along an alleyway on the hillside. When you come out into the open the Golf Club House can be seen down on the left. Follow the directions along the western wall of a cemetery, and straight ahead down to the road.

Turn right onto the road which you follow to the main Gloucester Road, where you go to the left. This will take you down to the High Street and back to the starting point at the church.

D. The church of St. Mary's is a memorial to the age of wool. It was built in 1632, but the wide nave and tower are earlier, having been erected between 1480 and 1490. There must have been a church on the site long ago because the Doomsday Book records that 'Wyke' had a priest in 1086.

The impressive interior, with its pleasing east window, has so much of interest that only a few items can be mentioned here. It is very light and spacious with a lofty old timber roof. St Peter's Chapel has a fine tomb shared by three families, one of whom was Sir William Kingston (died 1540) who was Lord Mayor of London, and had the doubtful honour of having charge of Anne Boleyn at her execution. There are many memorials to the wealthy cloth merchants who lived in the sixteenth and seventeenth centuries. Take a look at the modern porch built in 1969. Painswick has a celebrated peal of bells, one of the best in England.

Alternatives

1a **3 miles.** Either half of this walk can be undertaken with two cars.

1b By using the shorter walk (E) one can enjoy a delightful route of about **3½ miles**. Start as for the main walk as far as Damsell's Mill, then turn and make for Damsell Farm in a north-westerly direction. It rises up to meet the main road at Paradise. Turn left and after a short distance a track leads to the inward walk coming over the golf course. This can be walked the other way round. If so when you descend the narrow lane to Paradise you will find the stile across fields just beyond a house called 'Lynton'.

1c If you would like a pleasant short walk of **1½ miles** you can park in a lay-by on the main road near the start of the Paradise to Damsell's Mill route.

Parking

This is easy, and has been described already in the commentary.

WALK TEN

Chalford to Sapperton: Golden Valley Route

Distance: 8 miles

This walk starts at Chalford, a small village some four miles east of Stroud on the A419 to Cirencester. There is a car park at the side of the main road near Chalford church, right where the walk begins. If this is full there are problems (see under **Parking**).

> **A.** The church is early eighteenth century with a small broach spire. There is a surprising lack of evidence of the usual generosity of Cotswold wool merchants — perhaps because most of them lived at villages beyond Chalford, such as Bisley, Minchinhampton or Sapperton.
> The lectern is by Peter Vaals, who had his workshop in Chalford.
> Although the bells are not in the same class as those of Cirencester, it is proudly recorded that 'on Saturday Nov. 30, 1889, the Chalford Society of Change Ringers rang a 5,040 of Granshire Doubles being 42 six-score each called differently in 3 hours and 5 minutes'.

Most of this walk is along the towpath of the now disused Thames-Severn Canal, which has little water in its tangled undergrowth. It is, however, easily discernible with its ruined locks and bridges. The walk follows the canal all the way to Daneway bridge where you will reach a minor road and a solitary inn. It is a most beautiful pathway through the woodlands along the slopes of the lovely Golden Valley. It is also the course of the river Frome which accompanies you along the route sometimes flowing on your right and at others being on the lefthand side. You will consider it a poor little stream until it is heavily re-inforced by the many springs that pour in from the hills and make the flood of water that powered twenty–one mills in bygone days. It is unnecessary to describe the way in detail for you cannot go wrong, but one or two features might be mentioned.

Baker's Mill is encountered after two miles along the towpath, with the reservoir on its eastern side (B).

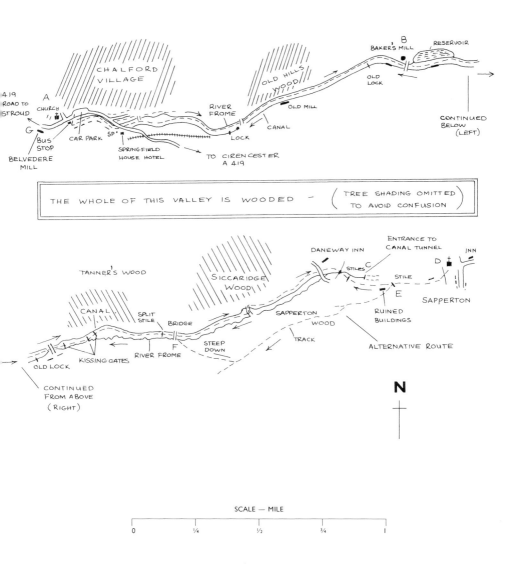

After 3¾ miles you will reach Daneway Bridge where there is an inn which can supply you with refreshment. However, you may prefer to finish the first half of the walk by going on the short distance to Sapperton which is attained by the short climb up a field path. There is another inn here. On your way you will have passed on the left (C) the entrance to the canal tunnel, which is 2¼ miles long.

> **D.** Sapperton Church is dedicated to the young boy Saint, Kenelm, whose shrine was at Winchcombe Abbey. It is a delightful building, full of character, with exquisite woodwork in the pews and panelling.
>
> The main part of the church was rebuilt in the reign of Queen Anne by the Atkyns family. Sir Robert Atkyns, whose reclining effigy is in the south transept, was a noted judge who lived at nearby Pinbury Park.
>
> The Earls of Bathurst, whose Cirencester Park stretches almost to Sapperton, have had a long connection with the church.
>
> The church registers show records of many men who worked on the great canal tunnel, which was completed in the late 1700s.

It was planned to have an alternative return route but public rights of way were only available for small sections on the southern side of the valley, which in any case is steep and difficult. It is recommended that

Chalford — Valley Walk

you return the same way, but if you feel adventurous you can try the route between E and F.

When you descend from Sapperton, at the end of the field path after the stile there is a well-discernible path to the left of a ruined building, which rises up the hillside. Turn right onto a track at the top and follow it for half a mile. Where it forks bear right down the wooded hillside. Here you will probably have difficulty because there are a number of apparent paths and none of them have markers. However if you make your way down to the river at the bottom you won't go very far wrong. You should join the outgoing path at the point marked F on the map.

G. In the heyday of the cloth trade the mills were a hive of activity. Some are gaunt relics of the past, but others are used today by industry. We discovered that one near the church (G) which is now occupied by an electronics firm was used early this century in the making of the film 'John Halifax, Gentleman.'

Alternatives

1a Numerous walks from **2 to 4 miles** along the towpath and back.

1b **4 miles.** One half of the walk either way by using two cars.

1c **3¾ miles** from Chalford to Daneway along this beautiful valley. Two cars required.

Parking

Facilities at Chalford near the church. If these are not available the position is difficult. The nearest official park is at Brimstone a mile towards Stroud. You would then have to walk to Chalford or await a bus on the main road.

WALK ELEVEN

Cirencester and Daglingworth

Distance: 9 miles

Although this walk is all on the level and really off the hills it contains so much of interest that it has undoubted claims to be considered a favourite. Cirencester was the second city of the Romans and it has a glorious parish church, and if one adds the Saxon heritage of two fascinating little country churches and the famous Cirencester Park of the Bathursts its total charms make the walk a 'must' for inclusion.

> **A.** Cirencester stands where there was an ancient British settlement before the Romans came. When the latter overwhelmed the Dobunni people in the first century they chose this ideal spot to dominate western England. It became Corinium, a fortified town from which they built great roads like the Fosse Way, Ermine Street and Akeman Street.
> The town's history can be traced at the fine museum in Park Street, which has some outstanding finds and constructions.
> Cirencester's greatest glory is it's church which was funded from the treasures of the Earls of Kent and Salisbury, and out of the wealth of the wool merchants. The town was a major 'wool' centre in the Middle Ages.
> It has a surprising amount of interest for its size – the extensive Park of Lord Bathurst with its incredible yew hedge intruding into the very centre, the Abbey grounds and river Churn, centres of art and crafts, hunting and well-known polo games in the Park.

The walk starts at the church from which make your way via Black Jack Street and Park Street past the great hedge, behind which Lord Bathurst's residence is hidden from the eyes.

Take the second narrow street on the left past a sign 'Swimming Pool with heated water'. For 300 yards follow a metalled path with a culvert running on the left. Cross over a minor road and after 60 yards a bridge, then 200 yards ahead you will reach a lay-by road round a garage leading onto the main A.417, where you turn left.

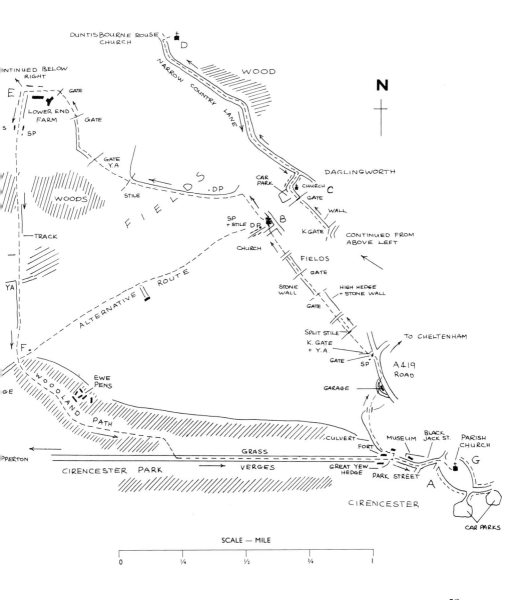

SCALE — MILE

WALK ELEVEN

After 350 yards, where the A.435 branches right, bear left through a gate, and almost immediately right through a kissing-gate. The way lies across the field, through a split stone stile onto a track. You will now move in a straight line for three-quarters of a mile as directed on the map. At point B, where the shorter alternative route diverges there is a small church. Pass through the churchyard to the right and turn left down the road. After a short distance there is a stile on the left with a signpost to 'Daglingworth'.

For the next mile you will traverse open and cultivated fields, on the first part of which the path follows the channel of a stream. Parts of this were completely dry when the writer last did this walk. At the end of this stretch is Lower End Farm with substantial buildings.

Pass through the centre of the farm, turning right at the end onto a minor road and almost immediately left through a kissing-gate. Cross the field with a stone wall on your right to come out by Daglingworth church.

C. The square stumpy tower looks very Norman but Daglingworth Church is a veritable sanctuary of Saxon work, perhaps unsurpassed in the Cotswolds. The south doorway, the wall sundial and four Saxon carvings (discovered in 1850) placed on the interior walls are a thousand years old. One shows a Crucifixion scene.

Duntisbourne Rouse Church

Cirencester Park

A brass memorial plate in the floor of the porch, dated 1638, observes that Jiles Hancox 'bequeathed his soul to heaven, his love to friends and £5 to the poor'.

There now follows a mile walk along a narrow country lane to the tiny village of Duntisbourne Rouse — perched on a hillside. I have tried to avoid roads, but this is worth the effort to see the tiny Saxon church which is reached down a grassy path from the lane. There is a sign on the left, but it so badly needed painting in the Spring of 1991 that it could easily be missed.

D. The beautiful, simple miniature church of St.Michael's is fully worth walking two extra miles to see. It is unique in its size — its box pews can seat only fifty people; there is a tiny crypt under the chancel which is probably Saxon.

It has a saddle-back tower of Norman origin and many other features. It seems very well cared for.

Return the way you came as far as Lower End Farm. In the middle of the farm turn right where there is a high stone wall to your left. You will quickly pass between two barns, going in a southerly direction. You will now see a signpost which would have been more sensibly placed in the farm yard at the beginning of the return route. Follow this track for 1¼ miles till you reach the entrance to Cirencester Park near Ivy Lodge. This is the point where the other end of the alternative shorter walk joins the main route (point F).

Although not a public right of way walkers are allowed in the Park. For nearly a mile you will follow the path through delightful woods until you come out on the main driveway, with beautiful grass verges. This stretches for five miles in the opposite direction. You will now be moving eastwards with the great church tower providing a majestic backcloth.

As you reach the end of the great drive you will pass the Fort on your left. The walk comes to an end as it returns to the church in the centre of Cirencester, and this is well worth a visit.

G. The vision of the tower of the great Church of Saint John Baptist has been with you for the last mile of the walk, so some comments are appropriate.

There was possibly a Roman place of worship and certainly a Saxon church on a nearby site where Guthrum was baptised after his defeat by King Alfred. Henry I founded an abbey in 1117 and a Norman church later replaced it.

The view down the nave is truly breath-taking, with its sense of size, light and beauty. The clerestory windows, especially the seven-light windows above the chancel are noteworthy.

There is a unique south porch, which is twenty-four feet long and has a rich fan-vaulted stone roof. It has beautiful carving, and is three storeys high. It is so large that it has been used for other purposes, including that of a Town Hall! The various lovely chapels, the fifteenth century glass, the wine-glass pulpit, and the Anne Boleyn gilt cup are some of the treasures you should see.

Alternatives

1a The walk's distance can be reduced to **7 miles** by finishing at Daglingworth on the outward section, and omitting the extra mile to see Duntisbourne Rouse church. (You can do this afterwards by car if you so wish).

1b If you find parking difficult you could use the quiet little car park opposite Daglingworth church, then do the circular walk from there.

1c **4 miles.** Starting from Cirencester, and omitting the part of the route which takes in Daglingworth and Duntisbourne Rouse. This involves leaving the main outward route at point B, and moving south-westwards to rejoin the main path at point F at the entrance to Cirencester Park.

Parking

Parking can be difficult in Cirencester. There are two large car parks near the centre — one has a maximum stay of three hours (not enough for the whole walk) and though the other is unlimited as to time it is usually full early in the day.
The small country car park by Daglingworth church is excellent if you wish to use it.

Hillesley:
Circular Route via Kilcott Mill
and Somerset Monument

Distance: 7 miles

A portion of this walk lies along a country lane, but it is so beautiful, with a profusion of wild flowers, that no apology is necessary. Indeed, the route both ways along Kilcott Lane is a joy, especially if you tackle it in May.

Start at the car park just round the corner from the Baptist church (Point A) and move off eastwards along Kilcott Lane. After a little more than half a mile you will be joined by the Cotswold Way coming in from the left and will stay on this long distance path for the next three miles. Shortly beyond this point you will reach Kilcott Mill.

B. The site where Kilcott Mill stands in a quiet secluded valley is mentioned in the Domesday Book. The mill was built in 1655, and looks today much as it did then — a long, greystone building with small windows and a wide oblong opening at the first storey through which wheels and component parts were moved in.

This was once an active corn mill, and has been a fulling mill. We were shown round by its private owner. The great wheel which drives the machinery is still in working order — we saw it rotating by water power as it did three hundred years ago. It is 18 feet in diameter and 7 feet broad, making a truly impressive picture.

There is a large pool above the mill controlling through sluice gates the water level and flow.

The roof of the mill looks old with its typical Cotswold stone tiles but, in fact, the original roof was dismantled in 1928 and shipped to America where it now covers a church in California! The present owner has restored it to its former glory.

At the end of the building was the manager's house, and up some wooden steps in an attic was a tiny room where the poor mill boy, probably aged about

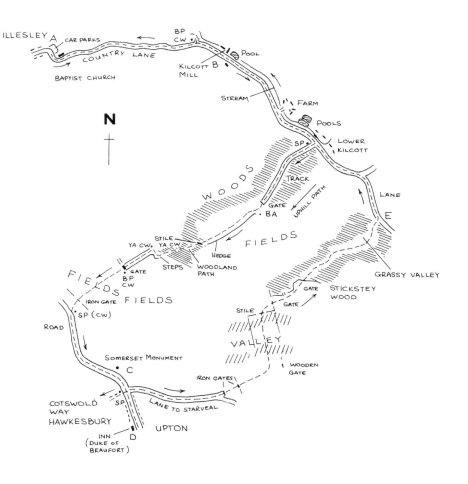

SCALE — MILE

0   ¼   ½   ¾   1

twelve, spent his nights in the dark plagued by rats and bats. So this idyllic place had its dark side.

The mill is not open to the public, but by arrangement the owner will show parties round.

Continue along the lane, past a farm, for half a mile when you will turn sharp right and follow the Cotswold Way up a rising track in a south-westerly direction. This goes for a third of a mile with woods on both sides, then you bear slightly right into open fields and follow the path with the hedge on your left up to the top corner of the trees. A stile leads into a short woodland path where you are directed by yellow arrows.

Eventually you come out into open fields where the way continues south-westwards till you get to the road. Turn left and you will soon reach the Somerset Monument.

C. The Somerset Monument was erected in 1846 to commemorate General Lord Robert Edward Henry Somerset, fourth son of the fifth Earl of Beaufort. He was an outstanding commander at the Battle of Waterloo in 1815. He died in 1842 and is buried at St. George's Hanover Square.

Permission is required from a nearby cottage to mount the 144 steps to the top, which offers superb views.

Kilcott Mill

The valley approaching Stickstey Wood

The walk now enters the straggling village of Hawkesbury Upton. Very shortly the Cotswold Way leaves you, turning sharp right at the pool on its way to Little Sodbury. You may now be in need of refreshment, so it is suggested you continue for another 250 yards when you can order your lager at the inn called 'Duke of Beaufort'.

D. Mine host and his wife at the Duke of Beaufort were kind enough to show me an old booklet about the history of Hawkesbury Church (nearby, but off our route) which has had connections with the Beaufort family of Badminton for a very long time.

The inn sign — a head and shoulders of one of the Beaufort's is notable.

I was also told that G. K. Chesterton and Hilaire Belloc used to stay at a cottage next but one to the inn. What a pity the latter (who wrote 'The Path to Rome') didn't write a companion classic called 'The Path to Hawkesbury'!

For the second part of the walk go back towards the Monument to where the Cotswold Way diverges. On the corner there is a signpost pointing to 'Starveal'. This directs you onto a lane going eastwards. Follow this for about a third of a mile when a short track on the left leads through an iron gate. After passing another iron gate you will be walking along the top of one side of a deep grassy valley. In about sixty yards turn sharp left, descend to the bottom and climb up the other side to a stile in the hedge. You may have to search for this as there are no markings or guide on this part of the walk.

Go diagonally across a small field through a gate and keep alongside the hedge for about two hundred yards when you will pass through a gate into Stickstey Wood.

Continue on this lovely woodland path for about four hundred yards, the last part going down quite steeply, when the way comes out onto a wide grassy valley where you turn right — moving eastwards. It gradually veers left and after a quarter of a mile reaches the lane at point E.

Turn left and follow Kilcott Lane for two miles back to the starting place in Hillesley.

If you walk in the Springtime there will be a wonderful selection of wild flowers along most of the way, with breath-taking sights of bluebells, cowslips and hellebores, not to mention carpets of dandelions — why should they be called weeds!

Alternatives

1a Short walk from Hillesley of **1½ miles** to see the famous mill at Kilcott, and back.

1b **5 miles.** From the Somerset Monument to Kilcott Mill and back using the Cotswold Way.

1c Using two cars walk from Hawkesbury Upton to Hillesley utilising either way round of the circular walk.

Parking

Accessible near the Baptist Church at Hillesley and at the Somerset Monument and Duke of Beaufort Inn at Hawkesbury Upton.
Kilcott Lane is only wide enough for one car so one cannot park at Kilcott Mill.

Nailsworth: Circular Walk via Avening

Distance: 6½ miles

A walk that offers the beauty and peace of the hills along the delightful Aven valley with its concentrations of woodlands and leafy paths.

The way starts from the car park in the centre of Nailsworth, identifiable by the clock tower. A few yards up Spring Hill the large facility is to your left. Only parts are available for all day parking, the remainder being limited to two hours.

> **A.** Nailsworth is not a typical Cotswold village but it has a charm of its own nestling down in the bottom of a bowl of lovely hills. It possesses a few features of interest — the old Quaker Meeting House, Bannut Tree Cottage and the Church.
>
> The latter is modern, having replaced an older building which had been affectionately known as 'The Pepper Pot'. It has a memorial to Nathaniel Dyer who, inter alia, left a guinea annually to the Minister to preach a sermon on the sixth day of February.

Go downhill from the car park (B), cross the main A.46 and pass the clock tower. A short distance ahead the road goes over a cattle grid, then you turn immediately sharp right and proceed along a narrow country lane, called Pensile Road.

Follow this lane in an easterly direction for about half a mile with the hills rising steeply to your left and the wooded valley below on the right. Through the trees there is a view of an old mill. A hundred yards beyond where the road turns sharp left a signpost points to the path on the right through a split stone stile where you descend steps down onto a woodland path. This soon leads down to the B.4014 road opposite the Weighbridge Inn.

Now turn left and follow the road for three quarters of a mile. This is not unduly busy and the beauty of the valley will make you forget you are on a road. Half way along you will pass the extensive buildings of Longford Mill, and beyond the river widens into a lake.

WALK THIRTEEN

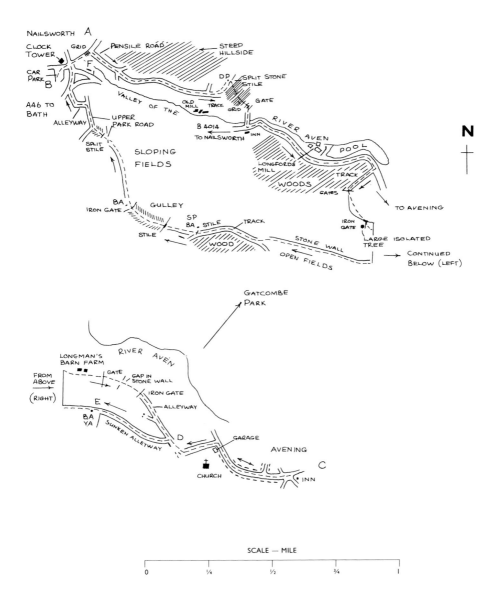

SCALE — MILE

0   ¼   ½   ¾   1

70

Where the trees on the right come to an end there is a track. Ascend this way and after 150 yards go through a wooden gate on the left and proceed across the fields in a south-easterly direction with the hedge on the right. When you reach the brow of the hill you will see a farm on the left, and the path crosses an iron gate by a large solitary tree.

There are no signs on this route but if you keep near to the right-hand side of the farm and go south by east you should find the stiles leading to an alleyway which will guide you down into Avening.

C. Avening is a most pleasant little place, which looks — and is — a Norman village, especially in its unique church, with its solid square tower, in an exquisite setting.

It is firmly believed that Matilda, wife of William the Conqueror, built the church, dedicated to the Holy Rood or Cross. Rectors are named from 1291. The same lady instituted a feast to mark the killing of a troublesome wild boar. The event is still celebrated on the Sunday after 14th September, when mine host of the Cross Inn has to supply sandwiches. The same gentleman showed me a letter from a Mr. Mullineux, a descendant of a French knight who was given lands at Avening for his assistance at Hastings.

On the hill above Avening is Gatcombe Park, the home of Princess Anne. The manor was built by Edward Shepherd, a great mill owner.

The woods in Aven valley

71

Bannut Tree Cottage

The north transept of the church contains an effigy of Henry Bryges, a notorious pirate and highwayman, who later reformed.

The return walk follows the outward path to start with as far as point D. Here you will diverge, following another sunken path in a north-westerly direction. This ascending alleyway comes out into open country after a third of a mile at point E. There you will see a yellow arrow pointing to the left (ignore this) and a blue arrow directing straight ahead. Follow this with a stone wall on your right for about half a mile, when the path enters a wood. After 80 yards turn right along a farm track, going west, for 300 yards.

Turn off this track to the right at a stile with a signpost and go across the field with a hedge on your left. Soon you will enter a gulley at the end of which an iron gate leads into a long sloping field. Follow this along the left hand hedge until coming out at a split stile. Go over the track along to Upper Park Road where you turn right.

A hundred yards down this road turn left along a passage leading to the main A.46 and 100 yards down you will reach the starting point of the walk at the car park.

This brings you to the end of what is hoped will have been a delightful walk, but there is one feature you might like to see before you set off home — Bannut Tree Cottage. To reach this go back up the A.46 for a few yards then turn left onto the beginning of the road to Avening (B.4014). The first part of it is called Tabrum's Pitch and the cottage is about one hundred yards up on the left.

F. Before Nailsworth existed and only a few isolated cottages stood in the wooded hills Bannut Tree Cottage was there on a spot quaintly known as Tabrum's Pitch. It was a 14th century chapel of ease. If you can imagine it without the subsequent additions it is fascinating to picture the tiny chapel built with local stone. It has the traditional Cotswold stone roof and original studded doorway. The blocked up opening above was probably a hayloft.

In its time it has been a chapel, a priest's house, a stable, a school and a museum. It defied destruction in 1558, and is now used as a cottage home.

Alternatives

1a Half this route can be undertaken to make enjoyable walks of about **3½ miles**. There is a bus service, though not very frequent, between Nailsworth and Avening, so half the way can be tackled without having two cars.
I think it is better to start at Nailsworth in order to limit the effects of gradients.

Parking

There are two small areas in the main parking places off Spring Hill for long stays. If you have any doubts they will help you at the garage. Most of the parking is limited to two hours.

WALK FOURTEEN

Frocester Hill:
Circular Walk via Uley

Distance: 5 miles

This walk starts high up on the Cotswolds to the south-west of Stroud at the Frocester picnic area which can be reached through North Woodchester from the north or Uley in the south.

The picnic area has toilets and large car parks. You will start walking due south, and almost immediately pass the Nympsfield Long Barrow.

A. The Nympsfield long barrow is neolithic in origin, having been excavated in 1862 and 1937, from the latter of which finds are exhibited in Stroud museum. Part of the end on the eastern side has been left open. Remains of between twenty and thirty human skeletons were discovered.

Continue ahead until you reach the panoramic dial, from which there are magnificent views across the Severn Estuary. On a fine day it is possible to see the Black Mountains of Wales in the far distance, and Berkeley Castle, where Edward II was murdered in 1327.

Follow the path for another 2/300 yards when steps lead up to the Frocester Road, where you turn left and in 100 yards reach the B.4066 road. Go along to the right and after some 70 yards there is a direction post marked 'Uleybury'. Here turn down into Coaley Woods. From the picnic area you will have been on the long-distance Cotswold Way and you will remain on it for the next mile on the woodland path.

There are no markings through Coaley Wood and it is possible to go wrong on divergent tracks. If you are in doubt take the left-hand path, but confirm by going southward with the aid of your compass. Towards the end of the woodland path there is an old disused quarry on the left, shortly after which you will reach the Uleybury iron-age hill fort, where the Cotswold Way goes off to the west (point B). Go out onto the road where you will see a direction post marked 'public footpath'. This directs one round the western side of the extensive hill fort, but the eastern way round is recommended as being slightly shorter.

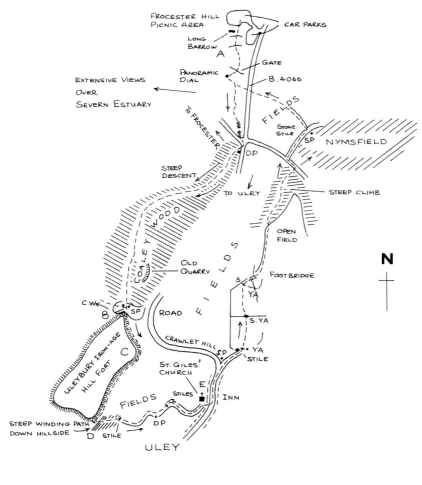

FROCESTER HILL
PICNIC AREA

CAR PARKS

LONG
BARROW

A

PANORAMIC
DIAL

GATE

B.4066

EXTENSIVE VIEWS
OVER
SEVERN ESTUARY

TO FROCESTER

FIELDS

STONE
STILE

SP

NYMSFIELD

DP

STEEP
DESCENT

TO ULEY

STEEP CLIMB

COALEY WOOD

OPEN
FIELD

FIELDS

OLD
QUARRY

FOOTBRIDGE

S

YA

C.W.

B

SP

ROAD

S.YA

N

ULEYBURY IRON-AGE HILL FORT

C

CRAWLEY HILL SD.

YA
STILE

ST. GILES'
CHURCH

E

INN

STEEP WINDING PATH
DOWN HILLSIDE

FIELDS

STILES

D STILE

DP

ULEY

SCALE — MILE

0   ¼   ½   ¾   1

75

The woods above Uley

C. The Uleybury Iron-Age hill fort was constructed more than two thousand years ago, and is the most spectacular in the Cotswolds. It covers thirty-two acres and in parts its steep sides are three hundred feet deep. A gold coin of the Dubunni people was found at the fort, which is now in the Gloucester museum, evidencing the occupation by the ancient tribe before the Romans came.

Now walk round the hill fort until you reach the far point at D, where you plunge down the hillside on a winding path through the trees. At the end of the woods pass a stile where you follow the path down across fields towards

Uley. At the bottom of the first field there is a sign in the corner which says 'To the Church'. Follow this round to the left.

E. St. Giles' Church, Uley, is very modern compared with the great ramparts above the village, having been built in 1858, but it is the third on the site. The first was Norman, a notice in the interior recording that 'Roger de Berkeley gave the church of Uley to a Monastery of Gloucester in the time of Gilbert the Abbot, 1139–1148. A Norman font is exhibited inside.

It was interesting to observe, on peeping inside the curtain to the Minister's vestry, a card with the quotation from Romans: 'How shall they hear without a preacher, and how shall they preach except they be sent.'

Turn left outside the church and proceed up the road, past the village green up to where the road bends sharply to the left. Now take the farm track with the sign 'Mutterell Farm and cottage'. On your way through the village you will have seen a number of cottages with typical Cotswold roofs. These are not done with slate or tiles but with stone.

Local stone is used which splits easily to make roofing slabs of immense endurance qualities. The unique style involves the use of five sizes, decreasing in size from the bottom to the ridge.

Walk along the farm track for about 250 yards when you will come to a house with a separate garage on its right. Between the two you will find a stile, with a yellow arrow. Go over this and proceed northwards. After two fields the path bears right and crosses a stream over a footbridge. Go left and straight ahead until you enter a wood over a stone stile.

Proceed along the woodland path for some 400 yards, the last section being a steep climb, when you emerge onto a road. Immediately opposite a sign directs to Nympsfield – ignore this unless you particularly wish to see that village.

Walk along the road to the left and take the next road on the right. In 200 yards there is a direction post pointing north-west over the fields. This will lead you back to the starting point at the Frocester picnic area.

Alternatives

1a **4 miles.** From the Frocester picnic area to the Uleybury iron-age hill fort and back via the lovely Coaley Wood.

1b With two cars you can do the short walk from Uley to the Frocester picnic area — **about 2½ miles.** There is, indeed, a bus service between the two places, but it is very infrequent.

1c The full walk can be done in the reverse direction, but this encounters some stiff climbs.

WALK FOURTEEN

Parking

Very ample parking available at the Frocester picnic area, and not difficult in Uley.

Kingscote: Circular Walk via Ozleworth Valley

Distance: 8½ miles

Within a few hundred yards of the start of this walk there is an inn on the A.4135, where bar snacks can be obtained, but there is nowhere else on the route for meals. This means that you will either have to do the whole walk in the morning to get refreshments at mid-day or take a picnic lunch if it is intended to spend the full day doing this most beautiful walk.

There is one other reservation that should be made. Part of the return walk, along Ozleworth Bottom, can get very overgrown with dense undergrowth especially in the high summer. It might prove arduous for a mile or so for the inexperienced walker, but well worth the trouble to enjoy the lovely woodland pathway. You are recommended not to wear shorts and not to take children on the return section, particularly in muddy weather.

If you want peace, tranquility and beauty then this is your walk. On a fine sunny day it offers escape from the bustle and wear of town life as you ramble through two delightful valleys with only a minimum of climbing.

The route starts at the village of Kingscote, where there is very limited room for parking. If space is not available it is suggested you seek the use of a large car park at the rear of Hunters Hall Inn on the main road.

A. For more than eight hundred years the Kingscote family lived in unbroken line at the Manor in Kingscote village. The churchyard has many memorials, some in Latin, to testify to national loyalty and long family continuity as country squires. At one time the Kingscotes were wealthy, with three thousand acres locally and lands at Uley, Ozleworth, Bagpath, Owlpen and elsewhere. The story now follows the pattern of many landed families whose position has been eroded by tax and changes in social trends. The Manor was demolished in 1951.

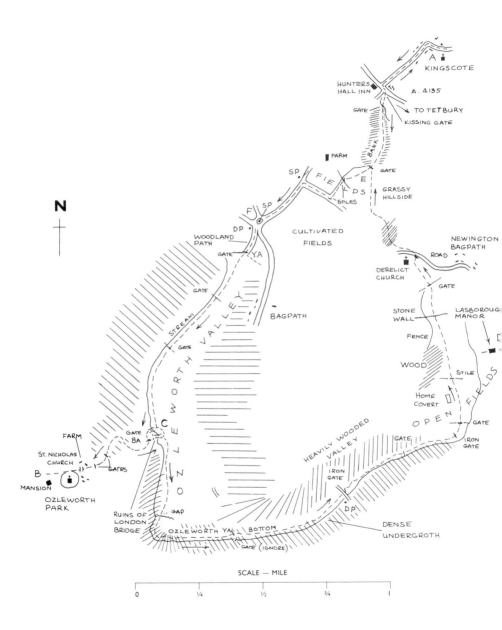

N

SCALE — MILE

0   ¼   ½   ¾   1

The Church of St. John, which revolved round the squires, was restored in the ninteenth century. Its most significant feature is a memorial to a famous man, Dr Edward Jenner, who was married to Catherine Kingscote at this church in 1788. He was responsible for the discovery of vaccination.

Take the way westwards from the church, then turn left along the tree-lined road that leads to the main A.4135. There is a bus stop on the corner, indicating the services available if required. Hunters Hall Inn is opposite.

Go left for 50 yards along the main road where you pass into fields through an iron kissing gate. After about a hundred yards take a gate into a wood where the pathway runs along a sloping bank. You will come out into open fields through a gate after 250 yards. In another two hundred yards you reach a stone wall — it has steps to enable you to surmount it with a small wooden stile right in front.

You now climb steeply up a large field keeping close to the right-hand hedge at the end of which a stile leads into a country road. Turn right, then after a short distance left where a signpost directs to Bagpath. Continue until you reach a signpost at the corner of five roads. Take the second left where after a few yards you will see a direction post indicating a woodland

St. Nicholas Church — Ozleworth

81

Ozleworth Valley

path in a south-westerly bearing. Just after leaving the trees you will find a gate with a yellow arrow pointing right which you follow into the start of Ozleworth Valley.

This lovely valley is heavily wooded, opening out a little after about a mile where a tiny crossing point has been made. The way along the valley is clear and easy to follow — in any case all you need to do is continue along the stream. At the crossing you go to the right-hand side of the stream and will see a gate marked with a blue arrow. Take the track which goes up steeply through the woods until you pass a gate and shortly another leading through an archway into Ozleworth Park.

B. The mansion is a fine eighteenth century building, fronted by a picturesque cedar tree. Virtually in its courtyard is a unique little church — as remarkable as you will see anywhere.

The church of St. Nicholas is Norman in origin, but has been added to over the years. Its outstanding feature is an irregular hexagonal tower placed right in the centre between the nave and chancel. Each of its six sides has a window high up under the eaves.

This tiny church seats only twenty-four worshippers but boasts its own miniature choir stalls and stained-glass window over the altar. The main arch is supported on two pillars with beautiful twisted stone decoration. The churchyard is probably the only round one in Gloucestershire.

Now retrace your steps back to London Bridge for the second part of the walk.

C. When I first saw this extraordinary sight London Bridge was an impressive stone structure over which a coach and horses could have been driven. It looked like a small edition of Sydney Harbour Bridge. Standing in utter isolation and spanning not a big river but a small stream out there in the wilds of Ozleworth valley it frankly looked ridiculous.

I was told that it once carried the main route from London to Worcester, and presumably coaches and horses must have passed over what was probably a much bigger river.

The bridge has now been partially demolished, but the four corner columns are still visible in the undergrowth which to-day buries the once elegant structure.

Cross over the culvert and turn sharp right so that you will be heading southwards down the valley. If you have any doubts about the way just follow the river for the next two miles, at first to the south, then eastwards and finally to the northeast.

After nearly half a mile go ahead through a broken hedge and soon you will turn left with the river to go in an easterly direction along Ozleworth Bottom. In a quarter of a mile you will be guided by a yellow arrow (ignore the gate to your right) and now the path begins to get less easy because of the heavy undergrowth.

In three-quarters of a mile a narrow track crosses your path where a direction post points the path through an iron gate. In wet weather this part of the walk can be muddy and you must walk with care through the forest until you come out into open fields in another half a mile when the way turns northwards.

Soon you will pass a substantial building up on the left at Home Covert. Continue ascending the grassy slopes, making for the right of the trees up on your left. You are now entering Lasborough Park and you will see the Manor over the small valley on the right (D).

At the top follow the fence round to a gate which leads to the derelict church of Newington Bagpath. Turn left at the road and almost immediately right where a field path takes you back to join the outward path at the iron gate marked E. The way back along the woodland path brings you to the main road and the inn.

WALK FIFTEEN

Alternatives

1a The first half of this route makes a delightful short walk of about **4 miles**, or a little less if you start at the inn. It will require two cars one at Kingscote or the inn and one at Ozleworth Park where a road gives access to the front entrance of the park.

1b If you prefer to avoid the less easy path of the return journey, but wish for an all-day walk it is suggested that you do the first half as set out in the description of this walk and do the reverse way from Ozleworth back to Kingscote for the second half. The distance would be about **7½ miles**.

1c **2 miles.** By starting at point F, near Bagpath the beautiful walk along Ozleworth valley provides a short route if you have two cars, or an enjoyable **4 mile** ramble if you are relying on one vehicle.

Parking

There is a small parking bay just beyond the church at Kingscote for about three cars, and vehicles can be parked on the short road leading to the main A.4135.

If these facilities are not available it is suggested you seek the goodwill of the innkeeper for permission to park at Hunters Hall Inn.